REORIENTING THE SEX TALK

KATHARINE L MCCARTHY

REORIENTING THE SEX TALK

FOR PARENTS AND TEACHERS

Sonora Mindling-Werling

Silver Sage Books

...when we speak we are afraid

our words will not be heard
nor welcomed

but when we are silent
we are still afraid

So it is better to speak...

A Litany for Survival,
Audre Lorde, 1978

CONTENTS

CONTENTS

LET'S NOT DREAD THE SEX TALK

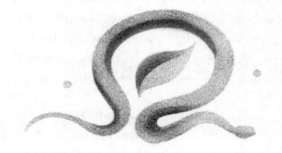

Talking with kids about sex makes us uncomfortable. Our discomfort makes sense. Sexual relationships are complex and potentially amazing and not easy to explain to young kids.

I taught Sex Ed for ten years. Being in conversations with kids and young adults about relationships and sexual intimacy pushed me to write this book. Reorienting the Sex Talk is an invitation to reconsider everything about how we think and talk about sexual relationships. We can help our kids become wise and wonderful sexual beings. We can be truthful and matter-of-fact about the complexity and nuance of developing and maintaining good, intimate sexual relationships.

We have to make some changes. Realizing new truths and changing deeply rooted ideas is challenging. May we be humble enough to be challenged and brave enough to change.

Here are five big ideas for starting this process.

1. We don't have to start these conversations by talking about genitals and babies.
2. Sex is about pleasure and so much more.
3. We can speak about the uncomfortable truths that shape us. When we don't, it's like teaching someone to fly without explaining aerodynamics.
4. We can claim our perceived truths while respecting our kids' truths.
5. We don't understand the sexual terrain of our kids but don't realize it.

First, we can talk about babies in the context of relationships because someone will be caring for that baby, and there will be a relationship. Eventually, we include specific information about potential sexual relationships that might be able to create a baby.

Second, there is pleasure and there is risk in sexual relationships. We can emphasize pleasure while also including risk. We can lead with information instead of with fear. We can even articulate our hopes for our kids' future lives - which might include sexual intimacy and sexual activity.

Third, North American culture is still firmly rooted in expectations of behavior - whether in terms of gender, sexual orientation, brain function, or ability. We treat people who carry babies differently than people who carry sperm. We teach consent as if power imbalances don't exist.

Fourth, our job as adults, especially parents, is to let younger humans teach us about their truth. Things are different for them, as they were different for us. We will be more useful when we listen carefully.

Fifth, once upon a time, access to information about sexual activity was relatively scarce. Now, it is always available in all its infinite variations. However, the most easily accessible information is produced for adult viewing, not for young kids learning about early sexual intimacy.

We really can talk about all of this.

Chapters 1 - 6 expand on these ideas.

Chapter 7 helps us think about the presence of pornography.

Chapter 8 provides language for talking about all of these topics with all ages.

Chapter 9 presents a few of my favorite ways of teaching the ideas in this book.

Chapter 10 suggests thinking about teenagers as brand new adults rather than big children.

This book reorients us towards understanding sexual behavior as a drive towards connection, intimacy, and pleasure more than a drive towards reproduction. When we talk about our hopes for our children's future, we can also discuss our hopes for good, strong relationships in their lives. Who needs a better sex talk? We all do. We can do this better.

Love cannot exist in any relationship that is based on domination and coercion.

bell hooks

CHAPTER

1

SEX IS NOT ABOUT BABIES OR BODY PARTS

Sex is about so much more than making babies.

Being embarrassed about bodies, much less sex, is all too familiar. Our embarrassment influences everything about how we conceptualize, legislate, think, and teach about sex. Without thinking about it, we assume sex means penis-vagina intercourse, and therefore, any sexual activity leads to pregnancy. We conflate sexual interaction with reproduction. Which then leaves us dreading any questions about babies from our young children. The dread isn't necessary!

Imagine a six-year-old asking, "Where do apples come from?"

What's your reply?

You probably didn't explain that bees pollinate apple blossoms.

Apples come from stores or a tree. If they ask for more detail, we offer it.

Imagine a six-year-old asking, "Where do babies come from?"

Why do we think we need to explain sexual reproduction?

Babies exist within relationships. Babies come from the body of a person with a uterus, and they grow up in a relationship with a caretaking human. We can talk about the skills necessary to create and maintain good relationships. There's a lot to talk about right there, and none of it is awkward or based on genitals.

Imagine a 10-year-old asking you how to drive. Would you explain the inner workings of a car? You'd find an age-appropriate answer, and if they asked for more detail, you'd provide it. You may remember your driving mistakes and bad outcomes, but you probably won't use them to scare your kid away from driving.

Imagine that same 10-year-old asking where babies come from. We are suddenly nervous. We are now thinking about our own sexual experiences - good and bad. We are uncomfortable with these adult memories as we face our young children.

But why?

How did we get here?

Why does it feel normal to us to be uncomfortable talking about bodies and pleasure and the possibility of creating life?

Why are we thinking about how babies are made when, in fact, we know that most of our lifetime of sexual activity (whatever it may be) was not about making babies?

How have we distorted our body's ability to feel pleasure and our ability to create life into a source of embarrassment or even shame?

All kinds of sexual activity amongst all types of people over a lifetime will be about sexual intimacy and pleasure, not about making babies. Most sexual activity between people whose bodies might make babies will involve attempts to limit how many babies they make.

Understanding the physiology of sexual reproduction is helpful, but why would we start there?

I taught Sexuality Education with my husband to kids and their parents between 2004 and 2015 near Seattle, Washington. Imagine seeing a little 6th grader cringe upon seeing you because you are the "sex ed lady." Imagine 7th graders pulling up their hoodies and trying to disappear during your class. Imagine 8th graders being visibly shocked to hear that "sex feels good. "

Remembering the dread on our students' faces and the "does sex hurt" question year after year woke me up to the significant problems with how we conceptualize and, therefore, talk and teach about sex.

My husband taught Human Relations at a small independent school for 20 years. We developed a Sexuality Education curriculum for 12-14-year-olds based on the Our Whole Lives Curriculum.

WE WERE BOTH COUNSELORS AND TEACHERS. WE EACH WORKED WITH KIDS WHO WERE HARMED AND KIDS WHO CAUSED HARM. WE KNOW THE KINDS OF MISTAKES HUMANS MAKE.

We knew that simply telling kids about sexual reproduction wasn't enough. We also knew that lecturing in front of a middle school classroom was not the best approach to this topic. Instead, we built in as much experiential learning as possible. We oriented our curriculum around consent. We created experiences that allowed them to recognize and communicate their boundaries through words or deeds. We defined consent as an ongoing, intimate connection, not a one-time, pre-sex agreement. We spoke plainly about covert and overt sexual harassment and assault. We answered their questions respectfully and truthfully. Fortunately, the parents and administration welcomed this. When there were concerns, we were able to discuss and alleviate them.

Teaching teenagers for many years and reconnecting with the occasional adult student kept me thinking ever more deeply about this topic. What information was useful? What harm still happened despite our attempts to prevent it?

These conversations with former students, our adult children, and my fellow older adults shifted the focus of this book from "How to teach better sex ed" to "Creating a very different sex talk that re-orients towards relationships and mutual pleasure while also acknowledging the presence of harmful cultural norms."

I couldn't think about the harm endured by so many without considering how our existing cultural norms allow this to continue.

My job as an author is to write about this in invigorating ways rather than pedantic, tiresome, or despairing ways. My job is also to help us have valuable conversations with young people so their life-long relationships bring them more joy than sorrow.

CHAPTER

2

SEX IS ABOUT WHO WE ARE

Who are you as you get older?

Who is this young person on their way to being an independent adult?

Our body, gender, sexuality, and behavior are all part of our identity. Let's sort out some of the confusion regarding gender and gender identity. Let's make sure we share an understanding of some basic terms. I consulted people who understand these definitions better than I do. Words in quotes are theirs. Any mistakes are mine.

Sex, Gender Identity and Gender

What's the difference between sex, gender, and gender identity? We mistakenly use them interchangeably, but there are important distinctions to understand.

Sex is a description of externally visible anatomical structures that someone records on a birth certificate based on the appearance of one's genitals. Sex refers to the visible differences between people who are designated female, male, or intersex at birth. Intersex is not a new medical category, but it is a relatively new term for most of us. Being an intersex person is a naturally occurring variation in human beings. Intersex describes people whose visible, external, anatomical characteristics demonstrate the fluidity of genital structures within human beings.

"Within the general practice of Western medicine, many intersex babies are defaulted to fit within the binary, commonly through surgery, commonly without the consent or even knowledge of the parents, which distorts our perception of the prevalence of intersex people."

Gender identity is how we know ourselves to be. It is how we feel inside and express our gender through clothing, behavior, and appearance. We may identify within a broad spectrum of identities, including but not limited to women, men, transgender, nonbinary, genderqueer, gender-fluid, or gender-neutral. Gender identity is deeply personal and may be fluid or static. Our feelings about our gender identity aren't related to puberty; they begin as early as age 2 or 3.

"Identity is the root. Everything else follows."

One might express their gender identity as transgender. A transgender person is someone whose designated sex at birth differs from their inner knowing of their gender identity. Their gender may or may not be evident to others. Some people choose to engage with a range of hormones and surgeries to assist in aligning their physiology and anatomy and perceived gender with their gender identity. The presence of transgender people is documented throughout history and across cultures.

One might express their gender identity as cisgender. A cisgender person is someone whose designated sex and gender identity are similar.

One might express their gender identity as gender fluid. A gender-fluid person is someone whose gender identity is variable over time and might or might not be similar to their sex.

One might express their gender identity as genderqueer or gender non-conforming. A genderqueer person is someone whose gender identity may fit within a particular label, but their presentation might not match some expectations.

One might express their gender identity as nonbinary. A nonbinary person is someone whose gender identity does not fit within the standard binary of woman or man.

The necessity of these careful distinctions arises from our cultural unwillingness to welcome human beings' abundant and beautiful uniqueness. These labels and descriptions continue to develop and change. They may eventually be unnecessary - not to erase the distinctions but to recognize the right and true place of all human uniqueness.

Gender is how we live into the truth of who we are.

"Gender is social and is expressed through behaviors, appearance, and interactions. Every culture has assumptions and expectations about gender appearance and expression."

SOME CULTURES EXPECT AND WELCOME VARIETY IN
GENDER BEHAVIOR AND PRESENTATION. OTHER CULTURES
DENY, IF NOT CONDEMN, ANYTHING BUT NARROWLY
DEFINED GENDER PRESENTATIONS.
GENDER CAN BE MORE OF A LANDSCAPE THAN A BOX.

Sex and activity

Considering all the things humans do and have done throughout time that are considered "sex," it's odd that we only have one word for it. The word "sex" has historically meant cisgender, vagina-penis intercourse. The word "sex" has also presumed the two people involved are fertile since we have oriented around reproduction.

On the one hand, who cares?

Can we say "sex" and agree that it includes all kinds of sex? No. Language matters, and we have a long history of excluding people through our language structure. Let's try something different. I will say "reproductive sex" when I mean "penis-in-vagina sex between people who are fertile."

I will often say "sexual relationships" to emphasize that sex happens within relationships. The relationship might be brief or lifelong, but sexual relationships involve dynamics of some sort. We also experience the dynamics of being sexual with ourselves.

I will also say "intimate relationships" to emphasize that intimacy might or might not be part of a sexual relationship. Sex isn't necessarily intimate, and intimacy isn't necessarily sexual.

Is sex about the survival of the species?

When humans were more nomadic, we carefully shaped the natural world for optimal food production. Even when some humans became more agrarian, we still carefully tended our environment for optimal food and shelter. We always needed more hands to gather and store food, fuel for heat, protection from human and animal predators, healing, wisdom, songs, and stories. Babies were welcome and contributed to the survival of the species.

While reproductive sex is undoubtedly crucial to the survival of the species, all the other sexual activity people enjoy is free of that burden. Humans have been having sexual relationships of all kinds long before we knew that a particular type of sexual activity might start a new life.

Which brings me back to an earlier question. Why has sex education been so relentlessly focused on the risks of reproductive sex when so much sexual activity has nothing to do with making babies? When did this norm get established? Who does it help? Who does it harm?

Gender and Behavior

We are familiar with the stereotypic categories of female and male behavior. We are also aware of the changing landscape of gender and gender identity. As we accept more fluid and flexible gender identities, we can also recognize more fluid and flexible behavior regardless of gender. While we do this, let's not completely dismiss the impact of our physiology on our self-image and behavior.

Anatomy

Our height, musculature, and body shape influence how we are treated. Walking down the street, a six-foot-tall person of any gender with well-developed muscles will have a different impact than a five-foot-tall person with more delicate musculature. Our response to either person will vary again depending on their race, class, size, clothing, gait, and attitude. While our gender certainly can determine our physical appearance, it doesn't always. Our presentation of self - clothing, gait, and attitude - certainly affects how others respond to us, inevitably shaping our perception of self.

Physiology

All humans and many mammals share a rich and varied blend of hormones influencing behavior. Stereotypically, we associate estrogen-dominant humans with bonding, feeding, and nurturing. We associate testosterone-dominant humans with individualism, athleticism, and even violence.

As we begin to understand the mistakes we've made in terms of sex, gender, and gender identity, we can also acknowledge the mistakes we've made in terms of stereotypic assumptions about gender-based behavior.

The structure and function of our bodies influence but do not automatically restrict our behavior. The hormonal influence of estrogen and oxytocin encourages the formation of solid attachments to the life of plants, animals, families, and communities. Strong attachments lead to a powerful urge to protect and provide.

The hormonal influence of testosterone assists in physical strength, stamina, and spatial cognition. While unusually high levels of testosterone are associated with aggression, testosterone levels are also known to increase in response to providing and protecting loved ones.

Humans experience a range of emotions and exhibit a range of behaviors. Hormonal influences, combined with culturally determined socialization, impact behavior.

"The evidence for hormonal sex differentiation of the human brain better resembles a hodge-podge pile than a solid structure. Once we have cleared the rubble, we can begin to build newer, more scientific stories about human development." Brain Storm: The Flaws in the Science of Sex Differences by R.M. Jordan-Young

Personality.

There is a dynamic interplay between innate and learned behavioral traits. When we observe behaviors, do we attribute them to a person's gender, genetics, family environment, or cultural socialization?

Let's remember many things can be true all at once and think about this differently.

Are some people more ferocious than others?

Are some people more tender than others?

Are some people direct and clear about what they want, while others are indirect and subtle? Of course. Let's help our kids understand this.

WE CAN HELP KIDS UNDERSTAND THEIR STRENGTHS AND VULNERABILITIES AND RECOGNIZE THE INFLUENCE OF ANATOMY, PHYSIOLOGY, AND SOCIALIZATION ON THEIR SENSE OF SELF AND BEHAVIOR.

Socialization

Let's think more about relationship dynamics we accept as usual and how they develop throughout our lives.

Our family dynamics throughout our early years shape our nervous systems. We adapt to whatever is happening and figure out how to survive and hopefully thrive. Our child-hood friends teach us our first relationship lessons outside of the family. These friendships prepare us for some elements of intimate, sexual relationships - the caring, the connection, and the fun, as well as the disagreements, hurts, and loss. But most of us spend our childhood playing with kids who behave and communicate in ways that work for us. We speak the same behavioral language - without realizing it is a particular language. By adolescence, we develop a strong sense of what others expect from us, even if we aren't fully aware.

Watch groups of stereotypically masculine and stereotypically feminine people. Are there differences? Are there similarities? Our culture validates assertive, if not aggressive, behavior in male-behaving people and accommodating, if not compliant, behavior in female-behaving people. Social expectations shape us. Relationships must navigate these. Talking plainly about this is essential.

An 8th-grade girl said: "Guys, friendships seem so much easier. If they don't want to do something with their friends, they say so. If I were that blunt with my girlfriends, they'd be all pissed off."

A 12th-grade boy said: "Girls speak in veils of meaning. I wish they'd say exactly and only what they mean."

Unsurprisingly, the communication between these two groups - regardless of gender identity - can be confusing.

Think about the behaviors society rewards on one end of the spectrum - cooperation, tenderness, sensitivity to emotion, and compliance. Think about the behaviors society rewards on the other end of the spectrum - competition, toughness, dominance, and aggression. Imagine these stereotypic but noticeable behavioral styles navigating a sexual situation. The male-behaving person will tend to behave in the familiar, habitual ways that work with their friends. Female-behaving people tend to behave in the familiar, habitual ways that work with their peers.

What are the chances of some miscommunication?

I know I'm talking about stereotypical gendered behavior. I don't include it because I like it. I write about it because it exists. Identifying stereotypes gives us more freedom to understand and explain them to our kids. They may or may not apply to particular situations, but it's crucial to acknowledge they exist and will impact their relationships.

Most of us have participated in some form of these dynamics in our own early and probably current relationships as well. Miscommunication can happen due to learned, gender-based communication norms as well as differing personal and familial communication styles.

**WE ARE ALL METABOLIZING OUR VERSIONS OF GENETIC, HORMONAL, ANATOMICAL, PHYSIOLOGICAL, RELATIONAL, AND CULTURAL INFLUENCES.
WE CAN ADMIT AND ARTICULATE THIS
AS WE TEACH OUR KIDS ABOUT
BUILDING SOLID AND NOURISHING RELATIONSHIPS.**

CHAPTER

3

SEX IS ABOUT PLEASURE AND SO MUCH MORE

_____

Sex matters for so many reasons. Pleasure. Power. Wisdom. Feeling comfortable with pleasure seems challenging enough for adults. How do we possibly talk with teenagers about all of this? How do we bring up pleasure and desire much less consent and sexual harassment? Let's see if we can reorient our thinking so that these topics become more approachable.

Pleasure, power, and wisdom.

What if we admit our awkward feelings about our bodies?

Being embarrassed about bodies, much less sex, is so familiar we hardly notice. What if we could think about our bodies as sources of pleasure and power?

Our bodies are sources of pleasure. They are also sources of power.

Imagine if we knew this in our bones. Imagine living even the next few minutes, telling yourself your physical being is a source of pleasure and power.

Just imagine.

Your body is a source of pleasure, power, and even wisdom.

It's simply true.

But we don't tend to experience ourselves like this.

Imagine if we did. Imagine if we could nudge young people towards comfort with their bodies as a source of pleasure, power, and wisdom. Feeling comfortable with pleasure seems challenging enough. Now imagine if the word power was not associated with power over others. Imagine if the word power evoked images of rolling waves, towering trees, or moonlight shimmering on the ocean.

Imagine if the word wisdom evoked a luminous stillness holding and guiding us?

Imagine if we spoke about sexual relationships as powerful connections between humans. Sexual relationships involve sharing nakedness and tender body parts infused with extraordinary amounts of nerve endings with another person. They also include sharing powerful states of mind and body.

Before humans knew how reproduction worked, we still had sex. Perhaps humans have had the same kind of sex (monogamous, polygamous, homosexual, bisexual, and heterosexual) throughout history that we have now.

Desire

Given that humans enjoy plenty of sexual relationships that are not about reproduction, what if we are hardwired for desire more than for sex? Perhaps it is delight in sexual activity that contributes to the species' survival. This delight could explain the physiological extravagance of female orgasm.

Are we hardwired for pleasure but confuse that with an assumption that we are hardwired for "sex," which we assume to mean heterosexual, reproductive sexual intercourse? Might more attention be focused on women's pleasure in sexual activity if there was a belief that female orgasm was essential for reproduction?

Once we think outside the paradigm of reproduction, what happens to our ideas about sex?

Hopes

WHAT IF WE START THE CONVERSATION WITH OUR KIDS BY STATING OUR HOPES FOR THEM REGARDING RELATIONSHIPS?

We might say something (adjusted for their age and degree of sexual awakening) about our long-term hopes for them in their loving relationships. We want them to enjoy intimate relationships in whatever manner works for them throughout their adult life.

Watch them cringe, get quiet, and begin to pay closer attention.

Expressing our opinions as rules, truths, and restrictions is not helpful. Expressing our views and hopes for them is powerful. Our kids may listen because, despite how it feels sometimes, they care.

We can state our opinions clearly but know they will make their own decisions. We can tell our kids that being sexual can be wonderful when they manage all the complexities. Then, we can do our best to help them understand and navigate those complexities.

We can be specific and positive rather than vague and negative. One parent might say: "I want you to wait until you are married before you have sexual intercourse. If you can't abide by this, please talk to me, and I will support you in making choices to be as safe as possible."

Another might say: "I hope you enjoy intimate, sexual rela-tionships when you are ready. I want to be sure you know the skills necessary to enjoy your chosen relationships fully. You can always ask me if you have questions or concerns."

One day, at the end of class, an eighth-grade girl asked, "How do you know when you're ready to have sex?" I am sure there are more thoughtful answers, but what popped out of my mouth was, "When you're ready to share naked bodies." She was a bit surprised by my answer (as was I), but in hindsight, it was a good one.

I was sitting at a table with a group in their 20s who knew I taught Sexuality Education. One leaned over and quietly asked me, "What's okay to do?" What a vulnerable thing to ask. We were in a Lutheran retreat center, so I imagined she was nav-igating her own decisions, given her family and community's expectations.

Sexual relationships are distinctive and complicated. We can experience incredible vulnerability, delight, and intimate bonding. We can experience boredom, shame, and disgust. I've heard sex called "naked fun ." I know of spiritual traditions that consider sexual relationships to be sacred and a form of prayer. Different people throughout time and all over the world have different ideas about sex. There is no easy answer for what is okay to do, much less with whom and when.

Some teens want to be intimate and sexual within one on-going relationship; others want to be sexual with many differ-ent people, and some want both at various times. Some teens will show interest in sexual relationships way before you want them to; others won't show interest until much later. While anything different from what we expected can be difficult to manage, this is our job if we want to maintain a life-long relationship with our adult children.

If we are lucky enough to be asked, we can help young people figure out "What's okay to do?".

When they will never ask directly, we can open the conversations. We can state our opinions and our hopes for them clearly and directly. We can assure them we know about the vast presence of online pornography. (See Chapter 7, Hard Truths) We can suggest online resources that are age-appropriate, accurate, and meant to educate more than arouse. We can leave this book or others lying around. (See Resources)

ONCE OUR CHILDREN RECOGNIZE THAT WE SUPPORT THEM IN THEIR CURIOSITY RATHER THAN TRYING TO STOP THEM, THEY MIGHT BE WILLING TO TALK WITH US.

Instead of setting up rules (to break or lie about) or pretending kids aren't interested in sex yet, let's offer questions to consider. They may or may not talk about their answers with you.

We can invite kids to consider these questions, but they should only answer them if they want to.

When might you feel comfortable being with another person with some or all of your clothes off, touching their body, letting them touch your body, allowing yourself to lose yourself in pleasurable sensations in the presence of another person?

When would you feel able to talk with a partner about all of this?"

Who do you want to be sexual with?

What do you consider "being sexual"? Be specific so you and your partner can be sure you're understanding one another.

What does being sexual with this person mean to you?

Do you know what it means to the other person?

What are your reasons for wanting to be sexual with this person at this time?

When and where would you be comfortable being sexual with this person?

Have you talked - in person - with this person about these questions?

What could you both do to ensure your safety and their safety, given that some forms of sexual activity could lead to pregnancy, genital infections, or transmission of other sexually transmitted diseases?

If relevant, what would you want to do if one of you became pregnant?

How would you handle things if one of you realized you had a sexually transmitted infection or disease?

As we all know, problems arise no matter how prepared we think we are. And talking like this in a new and exciting relationship can feel impossible. It's important to remember we aren't requiring anything. We offer words and concepts to help kids think about what they do and don't want.

In this chapter, I say more about "how" people do things than "what" people do. I am less concerned about what types of sexual activity people share and more concerned about how they share it. I care that people figure out how to communicate with one another while enjoying sexually intimate contact.

Good Lovers

A good lover is curious, attentive, respectful, and responsive. They know that different people enjoy different things. They are familiar with their desires and can communicate these clearly to others. They also respect their partner's desires, listen carefully to all forms of communication, and respond accordingly. They value connection, mutual pleasure, and mutual satisfaction. They are skilled at noticing nonverbal cues in themselves and others. They value the moment-to-moment practice of mutual consent.

For some, consent has become more of a buzzword than a helpful concept. For some of you, it may be a relatively new term.

Let's clarify:

Consent is not a pre-sex agreement. "You agreed yesterday, you can't say no today!" is an example of someone thinking consent is a pre-sex, irrevocable agreement. Giving one's consent to sexual intimacy requires a moment-by-moment willingness to participate. People's feelings and people's actions change quickly. True consent welcomes moment-to-moment communication and deals respectfully with unexpected changes.

Here is how we talked about consent with students.

Ideally, people share responsibility for clear communication in their relationships. Unfortunately, our world is far from ideal.

Dominance and Compliance

Imbalances in social status and power exist and impact behavior. Our culture grooms some people to be more dominant and others to be more compliant. While consent may presume everyone can request or decline specific behaviors equally, we know this is untrue.

Consent is only helpful if we consider the impact of these imbalances on all of us. We want to prevent our kids from causing harm or being harmed, so we talk truthfully about the relationship dynamics they will encounter.

In previous chapters, we noted that our culture tolerates and rewards dominance and greed. We can think about the specific ways this shapes our relationships.

Sex is not a competition.

The baseball metaphor persists - a home run being vagina-penis sex. When we think of a step-by-step progression towards a stated goal, achieving the goal becomes the focus. Once we believe there's a goal, we want to get there. Not getting there feels like a loss or a failure. Managing the thrill of getting to "home base" can be challenging without making a few mistakes. Did both people want to get there? Does getting to "home base" mean the same thing to both people? If relevant, was there adequate protection in place to prevent infections and pregnancy?

Sex is not a performance.

Sex is about mutual pleasure, satisfaction, sensation, and connection. Being sexual can be an invitation to be remarkably awake to the present moment in ways that maintain a connection with ourselves and with the other person.

We convey to young people that they can manage pleasurable and minimize risky parts. Discovering pleasure with another person can be as much of a meander as a run around the bases. We can approach sexual activity with curiosity, delight, and discovery. We can enjoy the tender process of kissing, touching, and exploring with no prescribed or expected destination. We can also enjoy intense, powerful, goal-directed sexual intercourse of all kinds. We can be sure they understand the actual links between pleasure and risk. (See Chapter 10: Our Favorite Sex Ed Classes)

Here in the United States, we do not provide much truthful, helpful information about being sexually intimate with others. We do provide infinite access to performative sex. A curious young person is likely to have viewed sexual activity online. What they view is designed to generate wealth for the producers by generating arousal and a desire for more. When this is a young person's first experience of sexual intimacy, it becomes a template for being sexual. (See Chapter 7: Hard Truths)

How does this shape someone's expectations of sexual activity?

Sex is many things to many people. Ideally, sex is about mutual pleasure and mutual satisfaction (whatever that means for the people involved).

Ideally, we also understand that desire for a particular version of sex doesn't guarantee we can have it. We generally understand this and behave accordingly.

When we go to a restaurant, we place our order, enjoy the food, and express appreciation. If the restaurant is out of what we wanted, we don't go into the kitchen and demand they make it anyway. We don't steal it off of someone else's plate. When we've been hanging out and snacking all evening with someone, we don't assume they are still as hungry as we are.

Whose responsibility is someone's desire for food?

Whose responsibility is someone's desire for sex?

Why do we assume some people's desire for sex requires others to comply?

Practicing consent may or may not prevent anyone from harming or being harmed. Talking about true consent does give people a place to start. It makes room for "yes" and "no" and "not now" and "how about this instead". It makes room for meandering. It makes room for people to remain connected as they roam around within the land of sexual sensation and intimacy. Ideally, practicing consent lets people be clear about what they know about themselves and what they want to explore together. Most importantly, practicing consent establishes the normalcy of people changing their minds from moment to moment. It also requires the practice of ongoing attentiveness to the other person.

Consent asks each of us to know and say what is true in each moment. We need to be more skilled at this, but we can learn. Consent teaches us to ask instead of being uncertain about how a partner feels.

We may be more used to complying with someone else's desires or to focusing only on our own.

Consent shifts our focus from performing or pleasing to aware-ness of our connection.

"Does this feel good to both of us?"

"Do I feel like we are both present?"

"Are we both experiencing what we want to experience?

"Did something change?

"Do they seem like they are on automatic?"

"Am I sensing hesitancy or withdrawal?"

"Did I say yes to this? Do I want to say no now?"

"I didn't agree to this. Now, what do I do?"

Ideally, we can all learn to practice consent. However, let's also remember the larger context of the culture in which we exist. Consent is impossible if one person has some kind of power - real or perceived - over the other. Consent is impossible if one person fears the other - for whatever reason. Consent is only possible when people can communicate (speak and be understood) and enforce (be heard and understood) their desires.

Consent when power plays a part

When there are power imbalances in a relationship, consent becomes impossible. Think about the power dynamics we navigate. There are social dynamics at a school or a workplace. There are teacher-student and boss-employee relationships in which one person's grade or salary depends on the approval of the other. Student-to-student power dynamics arise when there are differences in age, grade, intelligence, athletic ability, and social status. Power dynamics exist within any social relationship, including lifelong and short-term sexual relationships.

These relationships are all infused with some dynamic related to the differing sense of personal power people may experience. Can the vulnerable person in these situations give consent, or will they feel manipulated by the needs and perceived power of the other person?

Consent is a legal term. In the eyes of the law, the more vulnerable person in these relationships (student to teacher, employee to boss) cannot give genuine consent because it is unlikely to be fully understood or completely free of coercion.

"I can't count the number of people in my office who have had to process the trauma of being forced, coerced, pressured, or guilted into physical contact they did not want. Who have gone into a dissociated state to endure an encounter with someone who never asked them what they wanted and was bigger than them, or more powerful than them, or more sober than them and

simply took advantage of their bodies without any true regard for their lack of desire. I wish I could say that the people on the initiating end of these encounters were all vicious psychopaths. Then we could all believe that it won't be our children doling out these traumatic interactions. But many of them have no clue that they caused this type of trauma. Because they think they are supposed to "initiate" contact or pursue a person until they finally say yes, or think it's the other person's job to scream NO at the top of their lungs if they don't want the advances. We must do better with this next generation. The key is teaching them how to assess another person's desire and get their true, enthusiastic agreement to move into physical affection."

Eli Harwood, MA of attachmentlab.com

Bringing up Consent

One way to open this conversation with a sexually engaged teenager would be to say something awkward while driving them somewhere. "I'm not asking for details, but I assume you are enjoying some sexual intimacy these days, so I need to say a few things."

They will likely assure you they know all about condoms and, if relevant, contraception and are being careful. You persist and let them know that's great and that you want to talk about consent. They will tell you they know all about that, too. That's also great, you say, and then you say something like this:

"I want to be sure you understand the ongoing consent process. There are clear legal consequences for mistakes, which are important to understand.

THE BEAUTY OF THE PRACTICE OF CONSENT IS THAT IT HELPS YOU AND YOUR PARTNER HAVE BETTER SEX. (YOU CAN REPEAT THIS A FEW TIMES UNTIL THEY REACT.)

Practicing moment to moment awareness helps you stay tuned-in to one another. It makes it easier to say, "I'm uncomfortable, I don't know why, but let's pause." or to ask, "How is this for you now?" Understanding the full complexity of consent also lets you be a helpful resource if a friend comes to you troubled about something they've done or something that happened to them."

Then, you figure out how to talk about each of these topics.

First, talk about consent within an existing relationship.

You may feel comfortable touching or being touched in a particular way one day but not the next. Everybody gets to decide from moment to moment what is comfortable. You have moods, and other people have moods. Things shift and change between people over time, like with friends and family. You can change your mind at any time, and so can they. If you feel uncomfortable, figure out how to talk about it.

Second, talk about consent in more spontaneous, perhaps unexpected relationships. Consent is one thing when it's between two people who are in a relationship and have had time to talk about what they want or don't want sexually. Consent is far more challenging when two people who haven't established their relationship are sexual.

One person may assume this is a one-time interaction; the other may think it is the beginning of a relationship. They may or may not talk through what they do or don't want. They are unlikely to have the base of trust and care to manage discomfort or disagreement. Personality and communication styles are distinct and complicated. Some people's bodies say what they want without words. Some people hide true feelings out of habit. Someone might become quiet, turn away, or avoid eye contact. Some might giggle or begin to talk. Someone might move closer, begin to kiss, touch, or grab in unexpected ways. Some people will only know what they want or don't want once they feel how that particular touch from this specific person feels.

We may wish our kids would avoid more spontaneous sexual relationships, and it's okay to say so, but attempting to control their behavior will likely fail. Instead, we should prepare them for whatever they may encounter.

Third, talk about consent when intoxicated.

If either or both people are intoxicated, it is even more difficult to avoid confusion, if not harm. The likelihood of miscommunication increases significantly.

If these conversations are impossible, here's a letter summarizing all of this.

I offer this letter to parents or teachers who are very concerned about a young person's well-being and are uncertain about what to do next. This letter provides brief, blunt, accurate, information to help a sexually active young person avoid as much risk as possible.

Please use it as is or change it however you wish. If you are sure these conversations are impossible right now with your teenager, consider leaving this book and a few others around. I especially like Rethinking Sex by Christine Emba as an introduction to the current realities of dating. The author is about 30 years old.

I also like Erika Moen's books:

Drawn to Sex: Our Bodies, The Basics, Vol. 1, Limerence, 2018.

Drawn to Sex: Our Bodies and Health, Vol 2. Limerence Press, 2020.

Let's Talk About It: The Teen's Guide to Sex, Relationships, and Being a Human (A Graphic Novel) Random House Graphic, 2021

Also, scarleteen.com is Heather Corinna's incredibly well-informed and thorough website for young people.

If you are concerned about your teenager's sexual activity right now but can't imagine a conversation, this letter and these resources may help.

Dear _____,

I want you to be able to enjoy sexual relationships.

Sexual relationships are potent and pleasurable and potentially risky, but so are lots of things. You can enjoy the pleasurable parts and minimize the risky parts. I'm breaking it down here in terms of how much risk and how much pleasure is possible with various sexual activities.

Lower Risk and High Pleasure: *You know that orgasm is the peak of sexual pleasure. You may know that orgasm can be very different for different people. I encourage you to learn about the differences between people with a penis and people with a vulva. Search scarleteen.com for orgasm.*

You may also know that it is pretty standard for people to have orgasms without having penis-in-body intercourse. Fingers, hands, and mouths can stimulate orgasm.

Here is a simple guideline for avoiding pregnancy and infections:

1. *Enjoy the pleasurable ways to be together that may involve orgasm but do not involve the life-altering risks of starting a pregnancy or sharing infections.*
2. *Do not put a penis into another person's body anywhere without a condom on the penis.*
3. *Do not allow a penis into your body anywhere (vagina, anus, mouth) without a condom on the penis.*

Search scarleteen.com or plannedparenthood.com for more information.

Higher Risk and High Pleasure: *If you are going to enjoy penis-in-body sexual activity, it's even more important to be proficient with consent and condoms.*

Consent: *Consent is complicated.*

First, you have to pay attention to two things at once: how you feel and how the other person might feel.

Second, you have to communicate your feelings clearly (verbally or non-verbally) while also attending to communication (verbal or non-verbal) from the other person.

Third, you have to change your action based on that communication. If you realize your partner is uncomfortable, you know how to pause, adjust, or stop. If you are uncomfortable, you know how to make your partner pause, adjust, or stop.

If you can do those three things, making pre-sex agreements is still a good idea.

If you can't do those three things, you must make pre-sex agreements. You should also know those agreements can change at any moment.

Assuming the sexual activity you've seen online is "what people do" is a big mistake.

Assuming someone wants to do what you want - without asking them - is a dangerous mistake.

Assuming someone knows what you want to do and not do - without telling them - is also a dangerous mistake.

Be aware of legal definitions around failing to respond when someone asks you to stop, or you ask someone to stop. You can search for definitions of acquaintance rape, sexual harassment, and sexual assault.

Sexual Assault: *If you are uncomfortable with something that is happening and the person you are with isn't listening to you, I encourage you to be more forceful with your words and actions. Say "STOP". If that doesn't work, yell "STOP" and "HELP" as loud as possible. If necessary, use physical force - shove, kick, hit, run - to get them to stop touching you. If you have to be this forceful with someone, they are harming you and committing sexual assault.*

Condoms and Lubrication: *If you decide to have penis-in-body sex, know that contrary to what you might hear, condoms are wonderfully effective (98%) when used correctly every single time but less effective (85%) due to human error. Using a condom **only occasionally** is an excellent way to start a pregnancy or share an infection.*

Search plannedparenthood.com for the effectiveness of condoms.

Here is a big box of condoms and a tube of lube. If you're sharing these with your friends (or not), leave the condom box or tube of lube where I will see them. I will refill them without questions. Even if you are already familiar with condoms, please read the instructions carefully. Sloppy use of condoms is a common cause of pregnancy and transmission of STIs.

If the person with the penis declines the use of the condom, you can decline participation. If you are a person with a penis, consider that wearing a condom might allow you to enjoy the sexual experience longer since it reduces the intensity. If someone doesn't want to use a condom, ask why. I hope you would insist on using a condom every time, for both of your sakes. Practice putting on a condom, no matter your genitals. Be good at it. That's why this is a big box of condoms, which I will refill without questions.

Chlamydia and HIV/AIDS: As you know, making a mistake with a condom might mean getting or giving a sexually transmitted infection. Some have no early symptoms but are easily treated with antibiotics. This is why its important to routinely get tested. Planned Parenthood provides this and its not a big deal.

Search on planned parenthood.com

Getting tested: Health care providers suggest you get tested every six months as well as any time you are having sexually intimate contact with a new partner. Please set up an appointment with Planned Parenthood or with our doctor. You will not surprise any healthcare provider by telling them you're enjoying a sexual relationship, no matter your age. They help young people all the time. Their job is to help people seeking contraception and treatment for STIs. Don't hesitate to tell them what is true and ask any questions. If you're over 13, they won't have to inform me. If I get a bill, I will pay it without asking questions.

Please use our doctor or a clinic where you feel comfortable to get tested for sexually transmitted infections regularly.

Here is the phone number of a sexual health provider near you:

_____

Here is contact info for local clinics: _____

Planned Parenthood is a national organization and will answer any questions. 1-800-230-7526.

Scarleteen is another excellent online resource about life, love, and sexuality.

I assume you and I will not be talking about this, but I hope this letter will make a conversation possible. Let me know if you would like to talk more about this with someone in the family, a counselor, or a healthcare person, and I will arrange it. Most of all, this lets you know I am more interested in your well-being than in maintaining rules. With love."

If it seems correct to you, deliver the big box of condoms, a tube of lubrication, plus the letter (or even this book) to the young person. You may disagree with what I say here, but still accept that this may help a young person avoid the most life-altering risks of specific sexual activity.

In some circumstances, this letter may lead to a conversation. Unfortunately, in some circumstances, it won't make any difference. Even if they ignore this completely, you have done what you could, and sometimes, that is all we can do.

Good sex matters for so many reasons. Imagine if we spoke about sexual relationships as powerful connections between humans. Sexual relationships involve sharing nakedness and tender body parts infused with extraordinary amounts of nerve endings with another person. They also include sharing powerful states of mind and body.

We do young people a considerable favor by introducing them to the wonders of intimacy and sexual relationships while accurately preparing them for the challenges. When we don't speak about all of this they navigate the world of relationships with their glasses fogged and their compasses skewed.

CHAPTER

4

IS YOUR TRUTH THE ONLY TRUTH?

The world looks different to each of us.

I see my truth.

It is the only truth.

I am blind to your truth.

What do I give up when I soften into your truth being real?

What do I gain?

We can think in new ways about all kinds of things. We can think differently about bodies, intimacy, gender, and re-lationships. There will be some undoing and, eventually, a re-orientation. We can do this.

Although the ideas in this book may be familiar to you, they require reflection and humility to absorb and integrate. We must penetrate our customary assumptions and consider the possibility of other truths.

We understand this idea. Shifting one's behavior and beliefs is entirely different from understanding the concept.

An example:

As the parent of a 16-year-old girl slamming against our rules, I "knew" I needed to shift my parenting approach from rules to understanding. I understood the concept. I knew our relationship with our teenager might improve if we could shift from "We have rules, and there will be consequences when you break them" to "We want to know the truth of your life right now. We will trade rules for honesty."

I couldn't do it. Understanding an idea is not implementing an idea.

My fear for my daughter's safety kept me from implementing a much-needed concept. My fear was rooted in the basic template of me, family dynamics, and living as a woman in the world.

While I couldn't acknowledge the raw anxiety at the root of my fear until much later, I could borrow my husband's perspective. I could allow his nervous system to be just as valid as mine. I knew he loved her just like I did. Yet he didn't shake with fear and anger when she wasn't home by curfew.

There were other realities besides mine, and I could allow them to be true. This allowed me to soften and let go of my useless attempts at control. It also allowed our daughter to speak more honestly with us about the truths of her life, improving our relationship.

I use this as an example of how layered and invisible our sense of what is true can be. Expecting to notice it is like asking a fish to see the water.

"What I didn't know is that if you experience something for long enough, it just becomes the background noise of your life."

D.L Mayfield, Substack, 2024

But we can begin to notice.

When conflicts arise, we can think and feel attentively and ask, "What's going on here?"

I will say and feel familiar things. Then, I must pause and hover over the whole experience in my mind and body. What is happening underneath all of what I see and feel?

Can I express my experience of this conflict in a way that is free of blame?

Can I be so humble and vulnerable as to say, "I notice agitation in my gut, and I am terrified," - even when nothing objectively frightening is happening?

Can I be so brave and bold as to say, "I hate when this happens. I am furious and have been for a very long time," even when what is objectively happening is a relatively minor thing?

Can I then allow the same freedom to the other person?

Can I let the other person's experience be true and real for them even if I don't like it?

Can I make room for each person's quirky experience to be their standard for normal?

Must I insist that my (sometimes unexamined) assumptions about 'normal behavior' are somehow more valid than another person's?

Do we tolerate "normal" simply because "normal" feels familiar?

Do we tend to orient towards and value cortical intelligence, muscular strength, youthful agility, and well-behaved emotional expression?

Can we also orient towards and value "limbic" intelligence, moral strength, agility in crisis and grief, and vivid and varied emotional experience?

Can we accept our own mistakes and misinterpretations of experience?

Even when we think we see clearly, we may not. Even when we think we know who our partners and kids are and what their worlds are like, we may not. Let's talk about this, too.

First, what feels normal, true, and right to the older person caring for a younger person?

Second, what feels normal, true, and right to the younger person?

Third, what feels normal, true, and right in their community and with their friends?

We want to be as curious as possible about all the factors shaping behavior.

What feels normal to us?

Where did we come from? How were we parented, and what are our idiosyncrasies? What do we expect from other humans and the world? What are our blind spots?

What are generational differences to consider?

My white, relatively affluent, college-educated parents believed that sex only happened within heterosexual marriage. Sexual relationships of all kinds were happening in their lifetime, but understandably, they retained their generational beliefs about monogamous, heteronormative relationships.

My white, relatively affluent, college-educated generation expanded those norms significantly. I grew up in the 60's and 70's. We may have freed ourselves up in terms of sexual exploration and sexual orientation, but we retained our generational beliefs about gender. And we absorbed our parents' judgment and shame about bodies and sex in general.

Our children's and grandchildren's generations are revealing a more accurate understanding of gender. They are teaching us to see beyond our perceived beliefs. We can spare them the shame, pain, and judgment we feel and do our work to understand their new truths.

Why is this so difficult for us?

What about our own idea of normal is so compelling?

When something feels normal to us, is that a useful metric?

I grew up in New York City but left when I was 15. Decades later, when I returned, walking up 9th Avenue still felt "normal." Is it?

I was a younger sister in a family of four. Two of us were outspoken, fact, and detail-based conversationalists. Being quiet and invisible at meals felt "normal" to me. Is it?

Spending vast periods of time without words and without humans is joyous for me. Is this normal?

We can do two things at once.

We can become familiar with and accept our particular quirks. We can also become familiar with and accept the quirks of others. We can noticing when these quirks work well for all and when they begin to cause problems.

Our quirks are personal, not universal. We can claim them but we don't get to impose them as normal. Which means we can respect our children and students when they tell us about their world-even if we don't understand. We can be curious.

What do we do when the other person's quirks make us uncomfortable?

How do we handle our aversion, disgust, rage, or terror in the face of other people's "quirks"?

What do we do when someone's behaviors are seriously annoying, much less troubling, threatening, or dangerous?

What do we do when our children or students do things we can't tolerate?

Do I need to accept everything?

Clearly and emphatically, no.

With friends, family, and partners, we begin with "Hey, this doesn't work for me," and we may eventually need to end particular relationships.

With children and students, we intervene.

We say in whatever way we can:

"Hey, knock it off!"

Or "That is not okay with me."

Or "We need to talk about this because I'm worried about your safety."

Whatever we say is what we say, and it's where we start.

When we can do this clearly and directly, we are more likely to preserve the integrity of these relationships. Which I assume we want to do.

These dynamics happen within families. They are tough. We may still feel all the intense feelings in response to what they do and how they behave. But with people we love, we ideally will figure out how to talk about even the most difficult emotional experiences.

As we know, this takes precious time, energy, and sometimes financial resources. All of which can be scarce while raising teenagers.

What feels normal to our children or our students?

Can we see them for who they are, not who we want them to be?

When we notice their different "normals," it isn't necessary to immediately comment on them or compare them to ours. We can notice. That is enough.

How do they process information? Do they want facts? Do they like stories and personal examples?

Do they seem to process their concerns out loud with you, or do they work things through quietly on their own?

What might their developmental age be, different from their chronological age?

Do they tend to be more transparent and direct about what they want, or are they more likely to put others' needs first and not even be aware of their own?

How do they handle any conflict?

Do they seem to be at ease in their bodies?

As best you can tell, as puberty arrives, are they maturing a bit faster or a bit slower than their peers?

What is "normal" within their family, neighborhood, and schools?

What do they see and hear and adapt to every day at home?

What do they see and hear and adapt to every day in school?

What are they absorbing without even knowing it?

What do they absorb about race and ethnicity?

What do they absorb about money?

What do they absorb about gender?

What do they absorb about human behaviors?

All of it.

Let's notice what they might be learning about sharing their world with others.

Let's remember we can talk about all of this.

The idea of normal accomplishes two things simultaneously. It includes and benefits some and excludes and harms others. Once we set a norm, we can compare ourselves and others to it. We can point out that many of our cultural norms amplify and enforce self-focused achievement, if not aggressive striving.

What do we wish weren't true about our world but is still important to talk about with our kids?

Do we want to help them see the influences of a long-established culture that does not treat people equitably?

Can we help recognize the presence of racism and classism in how we think, legislate, and vote?

Can we help them prepare for situations in dating and sexual relationships that arise from treating women differently from men?

Can we help them recognize that we honor and reward masculine characteristics while diminishing feminine characteristics?

What are their peers' expectations? What is normalized? Do we even know?

What feels normal to them at parties and when going out with someone? How do we ask without shutting them down?

Can we talk about how they are learning about sexual activity? Can we ask what they know and what they think of as normal? (See Chapter 7, Hard Truths)

Are we willing to include the potential hardships and actual dangers of dating and sexual interaction - without cloaking the entire potentially wonderful experience with a sense of dread or fear?

Each family, school, and parent will determine what makes sense in particular circumstances. I'm inviting all of us to let our sense of normal, true, and right be vulnerable to change.

As I said at the beginning of this chapter:

The world looks different to each of us.

I see my truth.

It is the only truth.

I am blind to your truth.

What do I give up when I soften into your truth being real?

What do I gain?

Until you make the unconscious conscious, it will direct your life, and you will call it fate.

-Carl Jung

CHAPTER

5

UNSPOKEN RULES

If we want kids to develop good sexual relationships, we have to talk about the forces that shape our behavior. We wouldn't expect a pilot to learn to fly without explaining aerodynamics. Let's examine our biases as we begin to speak with young people about intimate and sexual relationships.

This chapter is about the influence of societal beliefs on our relationships. I grew up on the privileged side of our socially constructed beliefs about skin tone and wealth. I am not writing about the catastrophic impacts of racism, classism, and religious oppression.

I am writing about other social constructs that influence behavior. As our beloved children enter into relationships that can be both the best and worst experiences of their lives, let's prepare them! When someone I love goes into the mountains,

I want them to have a map of the terrain and a functioning compass. I want them to know how to orient themselves. I hope they enjoy the journey, appreciate the beauty, avoid the misery, and prepare themselves to handle whatever happens. It is no different with sexual relationships.

Let's figure out how to discuss this specifically within relationships with people we love and trust.

We can point out the cultural distortions that shape us and the harm done. We can be angry about it and blame others for our misery. Eventually, we may see that blame is a shield. Blame makes the other person the problem, which frees me from having to see my contribution to the problem, whatever it is.

We can all think of situations in which one person indeed causes harm. I'm not talking about that. I'm talking about figuring this out with a long-haul partner you trust to join you in this work. When we do this, we can better help our kids recognize how culture shapes their experience of themselves in the world.

Patriarchy as we know it is the architect of sexism, misogyny, queer-phobia, and transphobia. Patriarchy includes them all. (Thank you, bell hooks, for this.)

Religions built on dominance and control instill fear rather than open curiosity about the nature of reality and divinity. Religions with a rigid patriarchal structure obscure the presence of mysticism at the roots of all faiths. (Thank you to many writers and thinkers for this.)

Capitalism itself isn't necessarily the problem. Greed is. (Thank you to Chris Newman. Author of First Generation Farming, @Sylvanaqua Farms.)

Following is a glance at the phenomena contributing to the unspoken rules shaping our lives. I am not a historian or a scholar, but I read their books. I have included some relevant quotes. I write this as a parent and teacher who wants the world to be sane. I want to speak the truth to the best of my ability.

How would each of these cultural phenomena look without their familiar distortions? Patriarchy could understand "fathering" as providing care and respect. Religion could include instruction on the nature of reality and an invitation to direct experience of divinity. Capitalism could focus on generating wealth for mutual aid.

We can aspire to something beyond what exists, but we must begin by admitting the unspoken rules we live with.

Patriarchy as a domination strategy.

"Keeping males and females from telling the truth about what happens to them in families is one way patriarchal culture is maintained... Most children don't learn what to call this system of institutionalized gender roles, so rarely do we name it in everyday speech. This silence promotes denial. And how can we organize to challenge and change a system that cannot be named?" bell hooks, The Will to Change: Men, Masculinity, and Love

Throughout human development, some societies organized themselves around caring for one another and promoting a mutually beneficial distribution of resources. Other societies organized themselves around the power derived from acquisition and domination. Sadly, most of us are far more familiar with a society structured around acquisition and domination. Once we live in a society where power and wealth are hoarded rather than shared, we must control anything that might impact our dominance.

Let's think about this in terms of centuries of cultural norms developed around supporting dominance and greed.

Some types of sexual activity can lead to babies. Babies grow up and inherit wealth and power. Suppose we believe that our self-interest is more important than our common interest. In that case, we control the sexual habits of wives and daughters to ensure that our heirs and, therefore, our wealth stays within the family and our control. Greed and dominance lead to taboos against casual sexual activity - at least for the people producing new life.

A person accustomed to managing resources - large or small - will likely treat family members as resources. They will exert control over sexual relationships that could create babies who will inherit. They will protect and control the person they depend on to bring forth heirs. There is nothing wrong with protecting and defending someone who needs and wants protection. The problems arise when the person being protected wants something different.

When this greed and dominance extends to people, people become property.

In both cases, the household and the kingdom shared a common model of subordination. Each was made in the other's image, with the patriarchal family serving as a template for the absolute power of kings and vice versa. Children were to be submissive to their parents, wives to husbands, and subjects to rulers whose authority came from God.

David Graeber and David Wengrow, The Dawn of Everything, 2021

Although this became the norm, archeological data shows that living well outside a dominant structure was possible.

During the past 5,000 years "our conventional vision of world history is a chequerboard of cities, empires, and kingdoms, but in fact, for most of this period, these were exceptional islands of political hierarchy, surrounded by much larger territories whose inhabitants, if visible at all to historians' eyes are...people who systematically avoided fixed, overarching systems of authority."

David Graeber and David Wengrow, The Dawn of Everything, 2021

In the context of sexual relationships, imposing demands on someone who can't safely refuse creates these familiar unspoken rules.

Sexual curiosity becomes evil. Virginity becomes a virtue. Young girls are married off before puberty to ensure virginity. Forced marriages strengthen a dynasty. Love or attraction that can't produce heirs becomes taboo.

Women are stoned or burned to death for adultery or any other perceived deviance with no consequences for the adulterer or rapist.

Currently, we tolerate virginity pledges, abstinence-only sex education, restrictive abortion laws, double standards about sexual behavior, and the astounding prevalence of sexual coercion and assault.

All of that.

Why do we control female-bodied people but not male-bodied people? It defies logic to control the person who can only produce one new life each year. A young female in a family could optimally produce one baby per year. A young male in a family could quickly start hundreds of heirs in one year. Why wouldn't the man in charge of the wealth control the person who could bankrupt him by creating hundreds of heirs? Why weren't young men locked up in towers and shamed for their desire to enjoy sex? Why haven't we developed ways to control sperm production?

The person whose body can bring new life into the world is crucial to humanity's health and well-being. Humanity should structure society to optimize the health and well-being of the people who guarantee the continuation of the species.

Instead, we decided to control the female-bodied people. Why is that? Perhaps because we could.

Compliance as a survival strategy

A person accustomed to being managed - as a child or as property - will do whatever is needed to survive. Their survival requires compliance. We are familiar with trauma responses of fight or flight. We also recognize "freezing" and "fawning." Both will be seen as compliance but are a response to fear.

Greed exerts its influence on sexual relationships, especially those that could lead to reproduction. We all suffer from greed, whether our own or that of others. Some of us suffer far more than others. Greed drives our wars and our economy and creates the vast income gap we all live with.

As greed is rewarded, power is granted.

The Buddhists call this grasping. Catholics call it avarice. We all do it in particular ways.

Religion can function as yet another domination strategy. It has a long history of influencing society's norms to control human behavior. Religious leaders want to influence our behavior, which is fine. We need help to love our neighbors or to understand the nature of suffering. However, help differs from control, which requires some degree of force. Control becomes domination when enforced with fear and when exerted differently on different groups of people.

As written language develops, we record wisdom stories in the language of the people who have the power to create books. We hear, interpret, and translate oral stories into the language of someone able to sit and write all day rather than someone who must labor to provide food and shelter for others.

Who does the telling? Who can safely roam the world carrying myth and wisdom stories?

Whose words and beliefs are respected?

As vast tribes of humans continue to interact—through communities, commerce, and conquering—scholars translate these stories of myth and wisdom from one language to another.

Who are the scholars transforming dynamic, oral narratives into static, written words?

Despite a few exceptions, men were primarily travelers, scholars, monks, or patrons wealthy enough to produce books. The monks were beholden to the church. What was their perspective on sex, women, and power, and how might this influence their translation and interpretation of ancient myths and wisdom stories? To whom were they accountable for their survival?

All our foundational religious stories come to us through thousands of years of our fellow human beings' interpretations. We continue interpreting them however we want, making things up to suit our needs. That is all.

I understand from Rabbi Jesus - the carrier of myth and wisdom with whom I am most familiar - that his most heartfelt plea to us was to "Love God with all your heart, soul and mind." and "Love your neighbor as yourself." These would improve our intimate sexual relationships substantially if we spent a lifetime practicing them.

NOTHING ABOUT A SPIRITUAL PRACTICE BASED ON "LOVING GOD" OR "LOVING ONE'S NEIGHBOR" SAYS ANYTHING IN PARTICULAR ABOUT VIRGINITY, CHASTITY, MONOGAMY, OR HETERONORMATIVE RELATIONSHIPS.

While there are Biblical references to specific sexual activities, there are also references to particular fibers, foods, and behaviors that we happily dismiss as antiquated. There are only a few instructions about who should or should not touch whose body, when, or how. They tend to be more about incest and hospitality taboos. Yet, most of us have absorbed the idea that this young, ferociously kind, renegade wise man who roamed about with an undefined family of women and men thought sex of all types was terrible. We also absorb a convoluted notion that his execution 2,000 years ago should somehow impact our behavior, if not our soul, now.

When we don't wonder how these stories came to us, we believe that God and Jesus oppose everything except married, virginal, and heterosexual sex that might create a baby. We also think that making mistakes in our sexual activity will condemn us to eternal burning somewhere.

Once thousands of years beyond the original teacher, the critical thing to track is which version of the truth we are listening to.

Who decides which printed words to focus on and which to ignore?

Who is making the rules?

Who is served, and who is harmed by the unspoken rules?

Does everyone have to follow them, or is there one set of rules for some and another for others?

Let's test my belief that unspoken rules about bodies and sex influence us.

First, imagine you are young, unmarried, and sexually active. You realize something is wrong with your body. You wonder if you have an infection. Based on your symptoms, you think the infection is related to your recent sexual activity. How do you feel about this? What do you do next?

Second, imagine you are still young, still unmarried, and still sexually active. You realize something is wrong with your body. You wonder if you have an infection. Based on your symptoms, you think the infection is related to recent social - but not sexual- activity. How do you feel about this? What do you do next?

Both infections are likely treatable if not curable with readily available medications. How do you deal with the possible sexually transmitted infection?

How do you deal with the flu? How do you feel about being infected with each of these viruses?

Unfortunately, the ways we still think about sexual relationships, even in 2024, are primarily based on beliefs, norms, and rules that have deep roots in an unevenly distributed blanket of shame. This embarrassment reduces the quality and quantity of conversations we have about sexual intimacy with young people.

We don't realize that our familiar beliefs are entirely optional. We don't recognize how the insidious roots and flowers of our Western European thinking still permeate how we think, talk, and teach about sex.

We can discuss these ideas, but let's figure out how to live beyond the constraints and pain they inflict. Plenty of people are blazing trails out of this limited, harmful paradigm, and plenty of others are doing everything possible to maintain it.

We still reward bullying, bloviating, and dances of dominance.

Seth Godin 2024

You cannot enslave people or kill a whole continent of people. You cannot do that as a human being unless you have persuaded yourself that they are not people, their lives are not worthy, or that you have a mission to do that. No human being can do that. I don't know if that's malice or psychosis, but it exists, and the people who do it know it. They know that they are living a lie.

Toni Morrison, 1988

What is next level genius is telling young people that if they don't get all their friends and even strangers to get saved by "accepting Jesus Christ as their personal Lord and Savior" (but mostly just adopting a so-called "Christian" lifestyle), then those people are in danger of eternal torment. And it's your fault for not being brave enough to "witness" to them. I mean, there are generations of us out there who, at 14 years of age, weren't responsible enough to not leave our orthodontic retainers on a tray at Burger King, and yet thought we could be responsible for the souls of our "non-Christian" friends.

Nadia Bolz-Weber, Lutheran Minister and Theologian

CHAPTER

6

BROKEN RULES

We insist that willfully exerting power over someone more vulnerable than us is a problem. Yet, we allow it in our society in countless ways.

This chapter is about unwanted sexual attention that breaks the rules of basic respect and dignity.

Let's talk about it.

Grooming

I'm used to men expecting me to smile, listen, and be nice. I'm used to men on the street whistling at me or touching or grabbing me. I'm used to being interrupted. I'm used to men paying attention to my appearance but not my ideas and standing closer to me than I want. I know women who refuse demands for sex at the risk of losing their jobs. This is 'grooming.'

Grooming teaches us that our inner and outer worlds do not belong to us. When we don't adapt to the needs of those with power, we risk suffering.

How does this affect our early relationships?

How does this continue to affect our relationships throughout our lives?

"My feelings of safety running in the streets have always been unsteady. I've had cars almost hit me pulling out of parking lots. Men leaning out of cars have screamed things like bitch and cunt and cow and marry me. Which is truly the perfect encapsulation of misogyny."

Lyz Lenz @ Men Yell at Me on Substack

The nervous system of anyone experiencing constant grooming - of all intensities - becomes acclimated. Intrusion and even violence register as normal. My sense of "what is mine" to hold precious - personal space, thoughts, rights - becomes dulled and diminished.

This is a trained violation of personal integrity and dignity. This is trained compliance. This is grooming.

We tolerate male-behaving people ignoring, interrupting, belittling, and insulting female-behaving people. We also tolerate female-behaving people smiling, accommodating, complying, and avoiding conflict even if it means lying, much less being harmed.

I experience this through my gender. My white skin and suffi-cient economic status shield me from further violations.

Two essential ideas emerge here. First, we all tolerate both types of harmful behavior. Second, both types of behavior can be interrupted. Interrupting anyone's behavior is risky, but we can figure out how to do it with the people close to us. Both dominance and compliance harm us.

We can help our kids navigate this.

WHERE DID WE GET THE IDEA THAT AVOIDING UNCOMFORTABLE TOPICS IS A GOOD IDEA? WHO BENEFITS FROM THAT?

Coercion or bullying

We all recognize coercion in its elementary school manifes-tation - we call it bullying. In childhood bullying, there are clear cases in which one kid picks mercilessly on another until someone intervenes. In adulthood, there are more subtle coercive situations involving emotional, social, physical, or fi-nancial manipulation and responding compliance. Add sexual desire to this scenario, and the risk of coercion, confusion, and harm increases.

Teenage relationships involve people experiencing powerful changes within their bodies. Attraction and desire activate an ancient hormonal brew whose recipe has been refined over millennia to bring humans together. Each of us responds differently, but the pull towards some kind of more intimate, if not sexual, contact is powerful.

Imagine a high school in your community full of honorable young people whose judgment is still developing and adjusting to powerful changes. Remember that their physiology (male and female hormones) interacts with their psychology (a blend of innate and learned behavior). Each young person is hard at work metabolizing their own male/female nature/nurture cocktail while simultaneously finding their way towards mutually satisfying, intimate relationships. Managing this requires no small amount of social and psychological agility.

We assume if our kids manage well enough in their pre-dating friendships, they'll manage well in intimate or sexual relationships.

Most young people are awkward and tentative as they begin dating.

SOME KIDS WILL BEHAVE IN WAYS THEY'VE BEEN SOCIALIZED TO BEHAVE AND NOT REALIZE UNTIL YEARS LATER THAT THEY'VE BEEN HARMED OR CAUSED HARM.

Some kids will actively prey on their peers. We need to talk about all of this just as clearly as we might speak of the fact that some people will drive while drunk.

Here are some things to think about:

If our teenagers tend to be more straightforward, direct, and sometimes demanding about what they want, we teach them the importance of tuning in to subtle verbal and nonverbal cues from others. We remind them that just because they want something doesn't mean they are entitled. We help them practice accepting "no." We help them pay attention to non-verbal cues from other people. We discuss differing communication styles and the importance of understanding how different people communicate.

If our teenager tends to be more indirect, subtle, and sometimes passive, we talk about being very clear verbally and nonverbally about what they want and don't want. Some people will misunderstand their quietness. We help them practice knowing and articulating what they want or don't want in whatever way works for them.

Help them recognize behavior based on attempts to dominate and behaviors based on a willingness to placate. Help them be fluent in all this in its blatant and subtle forms. Help them learn to recognize and manage their tendencies.

Once we offer our kids names for both sides of a confusing situation - manipulation, and domination on one hand and compliance and placation on the other - it becomes easier to talk about.

Here are some questions to start conversations:

If you're at a restaurant and they tell you they're closing, do you walk into the kitchen and take what you want? If you did, would you understand that you are stealing?

If someone shares some of their lunch with you one day, do you assume they will share all of it with you the next day? Would you take it anyway if they don't want to share it?

If you make out with someone one day, can you make out again the next day?

If you're making out with someone the next day, do you now assume they want to do more than make out? Do you ask?

On the other side of those experiences:

If you loan your phone to someone one day and have to track them down to get it back, would you loan them your phone the next day? Why?

If you loan them your phone again, and this time they keep it, saying something about "deserving it" or "you let me use it yesterday," would this make sense to you?

If you're making out with someone and you get uncomfortable and turn your head away and shift your weight and try to move away, and they keep kissing you and holding you even tighter, would that be okay with you? Would you agree to meet with them again? Why?

As clear as we may be about borrowing or stealing objects, when we are sorting out dynamics between two people, especially around sexual interactions, we get confused.

There are people who cause harm.

Bad things happen. I don't need to tell you that. How do you want to talk about this with your kids?

We can start by using language that clarifies the actor in sexual assault.

Sexual assault is not an acute problem caused by pornography, bad parenting, or social media. Sexual assault is a chronic, historical legacy. There is evidence of it in any culture throughout known history. It is one more act of control and submission committed by people who can get away with it. The prevalence of sexual assault in the United States is awful.

"14 percent of girls, up from 12 percent in 2011, said they had been forced to have sex at some point in their lives, as did 20 percent of gay, lesbian or bisexual adolescents."

New York Times, 2/13/23

The prevalence of sexual assault within my friends and family might be shocking unless you've asked friends and family about it. If you have, you know that most women and some men have a terrible story to tell.

Is sexual assault a flawed interaction between two people?

Let's think about this in terms of how we might respond to specific situations of sexual assault between young people in our communities. When we hear about it, we may think, "Oh my God, did you hear?" We feel alarmed that a rape has occurred in our community (especially those of us who like to think our race, money, and location guarantee our protection). When we see a sexual assault through its very most minor 'frame' - as a flawed relational dynamic between one individual and another - then we will look for solutions, resolution, or revenge within one-on-one models. We would frame it as one bad actor harming an innocent person. Or as two people not being clear about what they wanted. Or even worse, as the vulnerable person somehow doing something to allow the rape to happen.

Is sexual assault an obvious outcome of patriarchy?

Our response might shift when we see this situation as part of a chronic condition of humanity. "Oh my God, someone with power used their power to get something from someone with less power." It has a different - perhaps more chilling - effect.

This difference matters. The first response is far more likely to descend into gossip. We will talk and blame even when we know we shouldn't and feel distraught for the people involved as we should. But we will need to place this event in the larger context of people with power, once again, exerting control over others because they can. We must also note that we've allowed more vulnerable humans to be groomed to enable this.

Once we can acknowledge the still pervasive existence of behavioral grooming based on vulnerability, we might be able to see the prevalence of sexual assault between acquaintances in our communities as a symptom of a much bigger problem.

Ethnic Genocide

We know rape is a weapon used to destroy entire ethnic groups by impregnating the women with an enemy's genes.

Stranger Rape

The stereotypical rapist is the stranger in an alley with a knife. The dynamics are generally evident. Someone attacked someone else and used their genitals (in addition to other weapons) as their weapon. While the incidence of this is statistically rare, the threat of it serves to keep vulnerable humans on constant alert. If you don't see yourself as vulnerable, consider the lifelong implications of this for the people who do. If you still think rape is sex, notice whose eyes you are looking out of. The rapist may think it is sex. It will feel violent to the body, mind, and soul of the person who is raped.

Acquaintance Rape

The prevalence of acquaintance rape enforces denial and silence. As I said earlier, it is as common as mud. Almost every woman I know has a story. When something is such a common experience, how do we help our children see the difference between an awkward, unpleasant interaction and an abuse of power?

Tragically, the statistically most common form of rape is acquaintance rape. This means within families, amongst friends, and obviously, amongst acquaintances (classmates, colleagues, coaches, priests, doctors, employers). Sometimes the dynamics of acquaintance rape are no different from stranger rape - someone penetrates the body of someone else without their permission. The difference is the two people have some existing relationship. For some reason, we don't think this is as atrocious as stranger rape. Once again, who is served by the false notion that stranger rape is more common than acquaintance rape? Who benefits from masking the excessive prevalence of unwanted sexual contact between acquaintances - often involving some degree of power imbalance?

Suppose we admit that the freedom to dominate and harm others remains virulent. In that case, we can figure out how to talk to our children, teach our students, and manage our societies differently. When we pretend we are over that - just like we tried to pretend we are over racism - we bind any attempt to make real change.

Let's look at acquaintance rape through the lens of two extremes of human behavior - dominance and compliance. People comfortable with domination may feel comfortable pressuring, harassing, and forcing their desires on others. People groomed to be compliant will tolerate pressure, harassment, and even assault for fear of behaving "inappropriately," much less angering the one with more power. The chronic existence of acquaintance rape is the consequence of a social structure that rewards greed and tolerates compliance.

Talking about it

Again, how do we talk about people who break the rules and cause harm without instilling fear in our children?

How do we help our kids be connoisseurs of both subtle and blatant behaviors?

We start by paying careful attention to our behavior. Then, we can notice our children's and their friends and family's behavior. There will always be examples of the more subtle types of boundary intrusions or even microaggressions.

Talk about all kinds of harassment - subtle, blatant, verbal, physical, sexual.

Discuss economic, racial, cultural, social, intellectual, and physical power. Talk about all types of behavior - unwanted attention, jokes, flirting, threats, sexual innuendo, casual touching, unwanted tickling, invasive touching, and physical and sexual assault.

If you talk about this, our kids are more likely to be truthful about their experiences.

Grooming and Harassment

Let's also discuss the more subtle forms of grooming, which we call harassment. Let's focus on the harasser rather than on the person being harassed. Let's call their behavior rude. That makes it easier to see what's going on. It's disrespectful when someone insists on talking to you, stands too close, or touches you in ways you don't like.

Some degree of persuasion may be reasonable.

"I think you'd love the movie. Why don't you give it a try?"

When persuasion becomes so persistent a person feels forced to comply, that's rude.

When the relationship between two people is unequal for any reason, it is especially rude (not to mention legally risky) to persist. It is also complicated to resist if you fear for your well-being, marriage, job, or health.

For example:

"Come over for a glass of wine after work, and we can talk about the promotion you requested."

"We're married. Why would you say no to me?"

Power can come from race, wealth, gender, size, intelligence, and social status. Differences in power change the relationship dynamics of any situation. What matters is how people wield that power. If that power is used to pressure someone into intimate sexual activity - as defined by the person being pressured - this can be considered sexual harassment, if not sexual assault, depending on the specifics of the situation.

Ideally, by talking about all of this, we help young people avoid causing harm and being harmed. At the very least, we help them recognize the impact of power imbalances in relationships so they can identify and talk about rudeness, harassment, or assault when it happens. Our job is to listen carefully and support them as best we can when they speak to us about any of these dynamics.

We can help young people distinguish between unwanted sexual attention that stops with a clear "Hey, Stop!" and unwanted sexual attention that becomes sexual assault.

We can help kids think about it like this.

When do both people's miscommunications result in a terrible situation for both of them?

When is one person's attempt to communicate being ignored?

At what point, does poor communication lead to assault?

If your kids are willing, ask them to talk with you about various hypothetical circumstances.

Ask them what they think happened and what either of the people could've done to avoid harming or being harmed.

"We didn't talk about it. I didn't want to, but I didn't say anything."

"We were drunk, and I thought they were into it."

"We talked about it beforehand, but later I said stop, and they didn't listen."

"We talked about it earlier, so I assumed it was fine."

"I said STOP and pushed them away, but they ignored me, and I couldn't stop them."

"I heard them say stop, but I thought they were teasing."

"I was at the party and went outside with them to talk. I am still trying to figure out what happened. I only remember waking up in my car in the middle of the night."

"They were flirting with me all night. We went outside to make out. I left after that. I have no idea how they ended up in their car."

Think about who has the power to change the outcome in each of these situations. Sometimes, it's clear; sometimes, it's murky. When we doubt the victim unless there are cuts or bruises, we are using the level of visible, external violence to determine the severity of the incident. We do not consider the emotional, spiritual, or economic harm to the person.

While our current legal system continues to be abysmal at prosecuting acquaintance and stranger rape, the social and emotional support and validation for young people experiencing unwanted sexual contact of any kind is increasing.

Sexual Predation

While most of their peers will be just as awkward and tentative as they are, some kids will prey on their peers. We need to talk about this just as clearly as we might speak of the fact that some people will drive while drunk.

I say it like this to students:

Subtle forms of rudeness between people can be challenging to recognize. Overt forms of rudeness, such as sexual predation, are violence.

If you're in a situation with someone and you have conveyed in every way you can that you want them to stop what they're doing, and they don't stop, you can break the rules of politeness.

When clear, direct words aren't working. The other person is now breaking all the rules. You must raise your voice and shout, "I said stop!". If that doesn't work, yell for help or yell loudly, "You are hurting me, get off me!". If yelling doesn't work, you need to kick, punch, and shove them away with all your strength. Focus on vulnerable parts like the eyes, nose, and throat (people with a penis will instinctively protect their groin but not their throat). Use any other type of physical force available to you. Tell someone as soon as possible what happened so they can help you figure out what to do next.

One of the more poignant aspects of teaching self-defense to more compliant people was their reluctance to use force to defend themselves. I encourage anyone who feels vulnerable to take a self-defense class. It can be a powerful, life-altering experience. It lets you practice shouting, punching, and using all your strength when needed.

If we deny our kid might be sexual, we can't teach them how to manage sexual relationships. If we pretend our kids aren't drinking, we can't teach them how to manage drinking.

WHEN WE TALK ABOUT THE BAD THINGS THAT HAPPEN, WE HELP THEM CARE FOR THEMSELVES. WE ADMIT WE CAN'T PROTECT THEM FROM HARM. INSTEAD, WE EMPOWER THEM TO DEAL WITH THE WORLD AS IT IS.

Intoxication and sexual predation

Generally, the best rule for anyone is not to get intoxicated at a party with people they don't know and trust. However, we know this can be impossible.

We can advise our kids to partner with a trusted friend. "Agree that one of you will stay sober. Agree to watch out for each other."

Tell them what you know about bad behavior. Tell them that older students often prey on younger students, offering them alcohol to render them incapable of knowing what they want.

Tell them that going into a room with someone usually implies an opportunity to be more sexual with one another. Don't go into the room unless this is what you want. Don't invite someone into a room without confirming this is what they want.

Tell them the hard truth that some people accumulate "body counts" and compete over how often they have had sex. "Having sex," in this context, has nothing to do with a relationship and everything to do with a one-time penetration of another person's body.

You can also say, "If you arrive at a party you thought would be reasonable and it changes and starts to feel uncomfortable, leave. Call us. We will be glad you did. No questions asked." You can set up a password they can use to let you know they want you to pick them up now!

*To fuck a woman is to have sex with her. To fuck someone in an-
other context means to hurt or cheat a person. And when hurled
as a simple insult ("fuck you") the intent is denigration and the
remark is often a prelude to violence or the threat of violence.
Sex in patriarchy is fucking. That we live in a world in which
people continue to use the same word for sex and violence, and
then resist the notion that sex is routinely violent and claim to
be outraged when sex becomes overtly violent, is testament to
the power of patriarchy. bell hooks, The Will to Change: Men,
Masculinity, and Love*

We must also talk about the miserable truth that some people
will carefully plan the use of memory-erasing drugs to render
their date unconscious. They will then use their genitals as
a weapon against an unconscious person. This is someone
to avoid. Unfortunately, they are not wearing a sign around
their neck that says "sexual predator." They are more likely to
appear attractive and charming. They are very likely to have
committed this crime more than once. When their friends and
the victim's friends begin to speak up, somebody will be able
to stop this behavior.

Repetition of this offense accounts for the high number of unsolved sexual assault cases - at least in our community. Many
years ago, a detective in charge of rape cases in my county said
they usually had 100 open cases they were investigating. He
also said that the young men they were investigating drugged
and raped multiple new victims. However disturbing this was,
it was a relief to learn that the reason for the high incidence
of acquaintance rape was NOT that there were hundreds of

young men actively pursuing sex with unconscious people. Instead, there were a few who were getting away with repeated assaults on unconscious women.

Think for a minute about someone who would carefully plan this. They have to select a victim from their acquaintances and invite them somewhere. They then obtain the drug, learn the proper dosage, and trick the victim into consuming the drug. They must be sure they are somewhere private so they can penetrate an unconscious person. Repeat. Assume no one will ever know.

Why won't anyone ever know?

The person doing this is getting more encouragement from their peers than outrage. Their friends and the friends of the victims fear the impact of making a public accusation.

We can talk with our kids about this. We wish it didn't happen, but it does. If they know it exists, they are more likely to avoid it.

You can say, "If you come home from a party and wake up the following day and begin to think some sexual activity happened that you do not remember and do not agree to, do something about it right away. Talk to your friends. Write down what you remember. If you can, talk to us. You may have broken some family rules; you may have been drinking while underage. These are minor problems to resolve later. Right now, the real issue is that someone assaulted you. If someone is intoxicated on any substance, much less unconscious, they are legally unable to give consent to any sexual activity. No matter what might have happened before the assault."

What can be done about it is another matter dependent on so many variables.

We can think about it like this:

Think about how you would respond if someone you knew punched you in the face. You wouldn't hesitate to tell someone and get medical care.

Why is it so confusing when the assault is sexual and from someone we were flirting with?

If they are concerned that they were drugged and raped, they can call a health care practitioner or their local hospital or a Planned Parenthood clinic and tell them what happened. They will know what to do. They will encourage you to come in right away before you shower. They will want evidence (there may be semen still in your body). Perhaps there's a conversation between families, with a lawyer, with the police, with a doctor, or with a therapist familiar with these situations. Unfortunately, rape cases are not given the attention they deserve and are often left unsolved and unpunished.

What if you realize a young person you care about is preying on others?

In interviews with incarcerated sexual predators, a researcher learned that many of them wished someone in their family had recognized the warning signs they exhibited. If you have any reason to think that your child might be targeting vulnerable (more naive, less able, less popular, younger) kids in any way, you must talk to them about what they're doing and the problems they face. You must also attempt to help them change this behavior.

Trauma in a person, decontextualized over time, looks like personality.

Trauma in a family, decontextualized over time, looks like family traits.

Trauma in a people decontextualized over time looks like culture!

Resmaa Menakem

CHAPTER

7

HARD TRUTHS

We can teach kids about sex.

We can do better than porn.

We can figure out how to talk about yet another hard truth.

Recently, a former student, now a young woman living in NY, asked to meet with me to talk about a project she was working on. At some point in the conversation, she was quiet for a moment and then asked, a bit tentatively, "So, you didn't grow up with porn?"

I said, "No."

She paused again and then asked, "So when you were first having sex, you just kind of figured out what felt good to each of you?"

I said, "Yes."

We both sat there, realizing how different our early sexual experiences were. I tried to imagine how things would be different if I'd watched other people having sex before I had my own experiences. She was trying to imagine being with someone and simply being curious about touching and feeling without any existing images of performative sex on her mind.

Those of us who came of age before 1990 did not have access to a relatively infinite display of actors having sex online. Instead, we bumbled through early sexual experiences - with the infinite variety of early experiences you can imagine.

Sometime around 2010, we noticed a change in the types of questions asked in the "Anonymous Questions" box in our Sex Ed classes. Before then, the questions kids asked emerged from their direct experience. We could answer them at the end of class without previewing them. After that, a few kids began asking questions we could only respond to by consulting Urban Dictionary. The 7th-grade boys asking these questions tended to out themselves with hysterical giggling when we answered. Eventually, we realized they were accessing adult sexual material online. We learned to invite whoever asked those questions to look up the answers on Urban Dictionary.

Here we are in 2024, and professionals are creating most young people's first perceptions of sexual interaction.

Viewing adult actors performing sex shapes a young person's perceptions of sex. This shaping is incredibly potent when viewed before they experience their own sexual interactions. When those perceptions are based on viewing porn that, by definition, is designed to sell, they are likely to include rougher and often violent sex. The violence tends to be committed by men against women, especially younger women and women of color. In porn, people don't discuss what they're doing, change their minds, use condoms, or have realistic bodies, much less realistic orgasms.

When this form of "sex education" is readily available, and better information is not, curious humans will view it. When adults don't know this, we sound like idiots if we stumble into some awkward conversation about babies or even safe sex.

If our first experience of sexual interaction is watching adult actors have sex, how does that shape our expectations?

Are we seeing two humans who may not even like each other being together in the most intimate ways possible? Wouldn't this be confusing?

Are we seeing people hurt and abuse one another?

How would this be different if young people could view people enjoying the delights of discovery? Or people awkwardly and truthfully figuring out how to feel and offer pleasure to one another?

When does a person's consumption of porn become harmful or an addiction like any other?

When does its powerful stimulation of the pleasure centers in the brain lead to sexual dysfunction in the viewer?

We can figure out how to talk about this just like anything else.

Younger people know what is true for them and their peers. They know they can view an infinite amount of sexual activity.

We can let them know we also know that this is true.

We can be curious and respectful.

We can distinguish between porn that normalizes rough or violent sex and porn that shows two people enjoying sex together.

We can express any concerns.

We can use the "Hypothetically" method of talking about the idea indirectly. "Hypothetically, if someone viewed rough sex online, might they think that was a normal thing to do?"

"Hypothetically, if someone was watching porn so much it was impacting their lives, what might they notice first?"

We want them to know they can talk with us, and if there's a problem, we hope we can help them think it through. Sometimes, we need to do more than this. Sometimes, we must say, "Hey, I think there's a problem here; we could talk this evening or sometime this weekend. Which would you prefer?"

If I were raising teenagers now, I would leave Christine Emba's "Rethinking Sex" around the house. I would also read Peggy

Orenstein's two NY Times articles listed in Resources at the end of this book. I would also ask other parents and peers how they discuss this with their kids.

You do not need to mimic everything you see in porn.

The majority of kids growing up today will watch pornography 2-3 years before their first partnered sexual experience. This means that most young people are getting at least some of their education about sex from pornography, whether they mean to or not.

And in a recent survey, more than half of young boys thought porn was a realistic depiction of the intimacy they would soon have.

The problem with this is that a lot of mainstream pornography presents a skewed look at human sexuality, often rife with misogyny and a lack of clear consent.

Porn teaches boys that they should assume a dominant, aggressive, and sometimes violent persona in bed. While this is a dynamic some enjoy, many men are deeply uncomfortable with this norm.

Due to the common lack of visible consent in pornography, they're also being taught to commit acts like strangulation, spanking, and anal sex without a conversation.

Much of mainstream hetero porn also teaches girls that they should grin and bear - or even express to enjoy - violence and that their pleasure is not a priority."

From @Teach us Consent

I wish this weren't true.

I wish people who haven't been sexual yet would not con-fuse sex between actors they've viewed online with their own exploration of pleasure and intimacy.

I wish young people discovering their bodies weren't compar-ing and copying what they see paid actors doing.

I wish everyone's first sexual experiences were affirming and full of delight.

Wouldn't that be nice.

We can't change conditions as they are. We can speak about what is true as calmly as possible and state our opinions clearly. Just like we do with everything else. At some ages, we can do what seems right to limit access to pornography. At other ages, we can begin to shift from control to willingness to listen, discuss and deal with truths, whatever they may be.

CHAPTER

8

A BETTER SEX TALK

Kids ask great questions. "Who would win a hurricane or a tornado?" "What is blue?" We might laugh or be amazed at their questions but find good answers. Parents and teachers know how to approach complex and important topics. We take a moment and think about what they're asking. We make connections between their questions and things they already know. We consider their age and personality. We do the best we can. We do fine with all kinds of questions until we hear,

"Where do babies come from?" Then we get uncomfortable.

Let's change that.

If you've read from the beginning of this book, you know we don't have to answer "Where do babies come from?" with a description of penis-vagina sex. We don't have to conflate sexual activity with reproduction.

We can talk about the skills involved in maintaining good relationships, much like we talk about the skills involved in becoming good drivers. We can discuss the skills necessary to create and maintain good human relationships. We can eventually tell them anything they want to know, but we don't have to start with heterosexual, reproductive sexual activity. Our job is not to answer one question once, nor is it to infuse anything related to sex with our embarrassment.

Our job is not to establish rules because these will change or be broken over the next few years.

We want to answer questions in ways that invite more questions. Ideally, we want to establish a pattern of age-appropriate, matter-of-fact, brief conversations in response to their specific questions.

Our job is also to convey that touching bodies and enjoying sexual intimacy stirs up mighty feelings. There are skills involved in managing these feelings. Sexual intimacy offers the potential for a lifetime of vitality and joy. Sexual intimacy can also make some unwanted outcomes more likely. We want to be sure they develop those skills and understand the risks.

We can also be attentive to our own responses as these questions arise and as our children become young teens.

What follows are all the big ideas, but this is not a To Do list.

You know these are complex topics. You've read about some of them in more depth in previous chapters. Please consider talking about them in ways that make sense to you when the time is right for you and the young person involved.

Acknowledge any embarrassment or discomfort. The parent-child relationship is deep and powerful. Whether we know it or not, we are sensitive to one another's inner emotional states. If we don't claim our own emotions, our child will absorb them without naming them or realizing they are not their own emotions. It is a mighty gift to our children to say something like, "I feel funny talking about this ..." or "You can probably tell I'm a little embarrassed, but I'm also glad we are talking about this."

We can describe our own experiences at the moment. This helps our kids absorb more of what we say and less of what we feel. The feelings aren't for or about them. They are ours. When we don't claim them, our children absorb those emotions and confuse them with the information. They don't realize the topic can exist without their parents' emotions. They will associate the topic (whatever it was) with the emotional load (discomfort or embarrassment). Discomfort and embarrassment are not the feelings we want related to sexual intimacy.

Many of us grew up with almost no useful information from our parents. We think telling kids everything all at once is good. But let's look more carefully and go about this gently. For some kids, talking matter-of-factly about bodies and sexual activity can be very uncomfortable. We may be talking about adult experiences before they even know what it is to be sexually attracted to someone. Answer their questions as precisely as possible. If they look miserable, we say, "Looks like that's enough for now. When you have more questions, you can let me know."

When we speak matter-of-factly about internal experiences like emotions or the changes that come with puberty, kids have language for what they're experiencing, which can be very reassuring.

Talk about the transformative process of puberty. Kids may bring up something that starts these brief, focused conversations. If this goes well, they may be willing to talk more about some of their concerns.

We can reassure our kids that people grow through puberty at different rates. Some start earlier, some start later, and some changes happen before others. It's all perfectly normal. They may have noticed differences in height or body shape changes among their friends. Girls talk about their periods, and boys talk about facial hair.

We keep our comments to a few simple sentences to establish that this is now a possible topic of conversation. We avoid focusing on their particular bodies or their friends' particular bodies. We speak in general terms about the process of puberty.

We pay attention and respect the cues they're giving us. If we start talking about this and they look miserable, we keep it short. Trust there will be another chance.

We can always leave an age-appropriate book lying around. We can say, "Of course, you can ask questions of the internet, but you may end up seeing things you'd rather not see. It's also important to rely on sources that want to educate young people rather than sources that want to entertain or frighten you. I'll make a few books or online resources available."

We're modeling respect for our child's particular level of comfort or discomfort, establishing a context for many more (possibly brief) conversations in the future, letting them know we are aware of the indignities and excitements of puberty, and caring about what they're experiencing. If we overwhelm them early on with uncomfortable information, they're less likely to ask more questions.

Talk about attraction in early puberty. Some kids will know what you're talking about. Others will not. We could open the conversation by saying, "I wonder if kids in your class seem to have crushes on each other." If that starts a conversation, great. If not, let it be for now.

Unless our kid would love to talk to us about all of this, it might be better to avoid asking directly, "Do you have a crush on anyone?" The less direct question about "their classmates" lets them educate you about their peers. It also spares them, the overly curious parents eagerly interviewing them about something they barely understand.

Another tempting opening line to avoid is, "I remember my first crush; let me tell you all about it." Some kids might be delighted to hear about it, others may feel embarrassed, and others may feel smothered by our stories.

These conversations are for them and about them. The point of the conversation is to normalize their experiences - no matter what they are - so they will be more at ease talking about them. This conversation isn't a chance for us to tell them about our experiences. There may be a time when they're older and may ask for more detail. But even then, we should limit ourselves to a topic sentence before launching into the complete essay. Even when they're adults, we're still their parents, and they may not want to know much about our dating or sexual experiences.

These initial conversations establish an open, respectful context for many ongoing conversations throughout high school and beyond.

Many people find they feel attracted to other people - similar to how you are drawn to certain people as friends but with more potent emotions. Some people don't necessarily feel that kind of strong attraction. There's a whole range of ordinary experiences.

Talk about variation in how and who people are attracted to.

If your child seems to be feeling that magnetic pull towards some people but not towards others, they may talk about it. It may be more difficult for them if they notice they are attracted differently than most peers.

Some people start feeling attraction sooner than others. Some people may feel intense feelings of attraction. Others may hardly notice. Sometimes, boys are attracted to boys, and girls are attracted to girls. Sometimes, boys and girls are attracted to one another. Sometimes, people growing up presenting as one gender may begin to express their true gender identity. Some people don't experience sexual attraction at all.

We get to say, "It's all perfectly normal," again and again.

Talk about touching in close relationships of all kinds. We can discuss (and therefore name) the type of touch and physical contact shared within a family, such as cuddling, snuggling, and hugs. We can also speak of holding and rocking babies and how some babies are happy with lots of cuddling while others are content with much less. It's all perfectly normal.

We assure them they already know about communication through touch. "We hold you when you are hurt. You move away when you're ready. We may hug or kiss when you come home. You may decide you'd rather not. This is all good. You may notice some of your friend's families are more or less physically affectionate than we are. You may feel like sitting closer to some friends and further away from others. That's all fine and good. It's important to notice these differences and respect them."

"When you're older, you may find that when people are attracted to one another, they enjoy cuddling, hugging, kissing, and touching that friends and family don't share. You may also discover times when you may feel attracted to someone but still don't want to touch or be touched by them. It is all perfectly normal."

Saying something like this is possible at the right moment.

"When people are attracted to one another, sometimes they simply want to feel that attraction and do nothing about it. Sometimes, they want to be close to that person and spend time with them. Sometimes, they want to touch that person because holding hands, sitting close, hugging, and kissing can feel good. Touching can be a way to express strong feelings of attraction to the person you care about. Touching can be a way to express love."

"Touching can also make some people very uncomfortable and can be used to control or hurt people."

"Sometimes, touching includes parts of the body that feel particularly good. You can decide who touches you and how they touch you. As you get older, we can talk more about this, and I will do my best to answer your questions as they arise."

Talk about managing their bodies for themselves.
You're helping them transition from a child whose parents determine what they eat and who they play with to a young adult who begins to make all these decisions independently.

You explain this. You give examples of how these things change over time as they grow into life as an independent young adult. You support their learning to be independent in all these ways because you want them to become independent adults - just not yet.

Usually, our conflicts with our kids are about when and how they become independent, not if. Perhaps you talk about giving them more responsibility in choosing what they eat or how they dress. You could talk about personal hygiene and body odors. You want to ensure all teenagers understand what's going on with menstruation. Perhaps you casually mention that male-bodied people may have orgasms in their sleep and that it's no big deal. It's a sign that they are in the process of transformation from child to adult. Perhaps you even say something matter-of-fact about discovering what feels good to them and use the word masturbation or make up a better one that doesn't sound so clinical.

Talk about establishing and recognizing non-verbal, personal boundaries. One of the markers for success at the middle school where we taught was if a child was able to manage their physical self as well as their emotional and intellectual self. Were they able to manage their body in space - not poking or hitting or stumbling over things - was one element of this. Another was whether they can manage their body in relation to others.

Do they understand what is okay in private and what is okay

in public? Can they control their behavior and their body in different situations?

Do they understand about personal boundaries and personal space?

When we talk about this non-verbal, subjective phenomenon of personal boundaries, we help them as they navigate attraction, dating, and sexual intimacy.

They become more aware of their sense of space around their bodies and more able to notice and respect other people's sense of space, however different it might be from their own.

We can encourage them to be aware of their discomfort when someone doesn't respect their sense of personal space. We can encourage them to notice if someone else seems to be uncomfortable with their behavior.

We can help them to notice how different people seem to have distinct boundaries. Some people like to stand close, others stand a bit further.

We can talk about how personal boundaries differ in different cultures.

We can help them feel and name uncomfortable feelings that are difficult to express. We can encourage them to trust those feelings and act on them. Many kids may not realize that an experience they're having is "a thing" that can be talked about with trusted adults until we name and talk about it. This is why we want to speak again and again about personal boundaries.

Talk about establishing verbal boundaries, saying yes and no clearly and respectfully. We can help them communicate in an honest and straightforward manner with friends and people they may date. I place a higher priority on supporting their preferences than on being stereotypically polite or nice. We want them to be clear and respectful to others as they learn what they want or don't want. Their decision may feel hurtful to someone else, but that is, once again, perfectly normal. We want them to be good at expressing their preferences verbally and non-verbally. They will need this skill again and again throughout a lifetime. We want them to be good at it.

We can tell them how important it is to be very clear - with their words, with their gestures, with their whole body - in dating or sexually intimate situations. We can point out the cultural norms of behavior. We can teach our kids that saying no is as important as saying yes. Knowing what they don't want is as important as knowing what they want. We can explain how being nice differs from being straightforward and that dishonesty in an attempt to be nice is confusing, if not cruel. We can talk about being transparent, honest, and respectful - without being insulting, condescending, or dismissive.

We saw this issue clearly during a particularly unruly 7th-grade class. Our planned lesson was not working, so we quickly changed plans and suggested they figure out how to ask someone on a date. To my surprise, they were willing.

We asked, "Would you ask a person out via text or in person? What might you say? Where might you want to go?" They went around the room, one at a time, each person managing to find words to ask someone on a date. They appreciated the opportunity to think about and practice this. There was even some peer feedback to kids who were abrupt, thoughtless, or muddled in their approach.

Then we suggested they figure out how to decline an invitation. "Would you do it in person or via text? What might you say?"

This class often sat grouped by gender. So, all the boys answered these questions first, then all the girls. We went around the room, one at a time, each person taking turns to figure out how to say, "No, thank you." Once they finished, we said, "Did you all notice any differences between the boys' and girls' responses?" They said, "Nope." We were out of time, so we dismissed the class.

We sat back, and we looked at each other with dismay. The boys had conveyed a clear "No" with relative ease. Some stumbled on being nice about it but could still decline the offer.

Every single girl in the class struggled. Some fidgeted, some were very uncomfortable, and were at a loss for words. They all expressed concern about hurting someone's feelings; many could hardly say no. In 10 years of teaching, we have seen these roles reversed, with some girls perfectly capable of saying what they did or didn't want and some boys struggling to do the same. However, boys were generally comfortable saying no, while girls were not.

Think about it!

We can help our kids feel comfortable and respectful about saying yes and no. They may need our help and support. Let them know that good relationships always require some work.

Discuss body boundaries in terms of particular areas of their body. We've discussed establishing personal boundaries in general.

We also want to speak specifically about extending this awareness to all parts of the body - what some may call "private parts. Perhaps we say genitals. Maybe we say testicles and penis and vulva and vagina or balls and dick and kootchy. Maybe we include butts and boobs. The specific terms matter less than simply talking about the body - in all its glory. What matters is that we calmly name these parts of the body and any other parts so our kids know they can talk about them. We want them to feel in charge of who does or doesn't touch them - whether it's an overly affectionate aunt or an unruly date. We may also want them to be able to talk about these body parts in some way or another with potential sexual partners.

We may want to acknowledge that perhaps at the moment (depending on their age), touching or being touched on their private parts with someone else may sound gross ("Eww, that's where I pee from!"). We can let them know that this may change over time. We may or may not also want to mention that exploring their own body in their room is fine.

Talk about consent in more sexually intimate relationships. We've established that it's natural to like some people better than others. We've talked about turning down invitations from friends or potential dates. We've established that we will do our best to support them in their preferences.

If our kids are already interested in dating, we want to talk about consent, specifically in the context of early dating. They've likely heard the word consent before and will be emphatic about their knowledge. That's great. We can humbly request an explanation since we didn't learn about it in school like they did.

(See Chapter 7, Broken Rules)

We want to discuss the difference between the desire to do something and doing it. Desire is not the same as action. We can reference playing a sport where players' strongest desire is to win, but they withhold specific actions that won't be tolerated. They've learned to control their full strength to safely and legally win a game. They will think this is a ridiculous analogy, but that's fine.

We also want to discuss managing strong feelings in a more intimate context. Maybe they've experienced tickling a younger sibling who seemed to love being tickled until they suddenly didn't. Or perhaps they've been tickled by an older relative and never really liked it but didn't know how to stop it. We can use these situations to ask questions and invite them to be curious about both situations. How might people feel, and how might they express their wishes?

It's vital to be sure the people you're doing these things with want to do them with you, too. We can articulate the importance of receiving a heartfelt "yes" rather than assuming silence or even giggling means "yes." We can do our best to talk about the ongoing, moment-to-moment reality of consent in any situation.

Maybe you say something awkward while driving them home, like, "I want to be sure you understand about consent. I want to be sure you know that even if you felt comfortable with someone touching you (or you touching someone) in a particular way one day, that doesn't mean consent is now permanent. You get to decide from moment to moment what is comfortable for you. As does your partner. You have moods. Other people have moods. Feelings shift and change between people over time. You can change your mind at any time. If the person you're in a relationship with doesn't understand, you might consider backing off and trying to talk more about this."

If they don't join the conversation, we may have to be quiet and hope for another moment. (See my blunt Letter to a Teenager in this Chapter)

Talk about passive, active, and aggressive behaviors.
Maybe you draw a kind of 'meter' on paper and write "passive" on the far left side and "aggressive" on the far right. Or you write persuading on one end and forcing on the other. Then, we can talk about how people communicate along the spectrum, from passive to aggressive. You want to stir up disagreement. You're hoping for an informative discussion about people's subjective experiences of the distinctions between asking, persuading, coercion, and force. Parents telling kids to do things is a perfect example of persuasion. We tend to have a rich vocabulary for encouraging compliance with rules. We can start the conversation there!

Talk about navigating unwanted sexual attention and contact. While most of their peers will be just as awkward and tentative as they are, some kids will prey on their peers. We need to talk about this just as clearly as we might talk about the dangers of driving when drunk. They need to know how common it is. If you have any reason to think that your teenager might be the person targeting vulnerable kids - in any way - you must talk to them about what they're doing and the problems they will face. It would be best to find ways to help them change this approach to their fellow humans. (See Chapter 7, Broken Rules)

Talk about sexual harassment and acquaintance rape. If you're not familiar with the prevalence of acquaintance rape in the general population, please learn more about this. Kids are always dumbfounded when we tell them that stranger rape is relatively rare while acquaintance rape is terribly common. When talking with kids, try avoiding familiar terminology like acquaintance rape or sexual assault. I try to refer to their direct experience rather than using a label. I might ask, "Do you have any experience of someone touching you in ways you didn't like?" or "Have you been disappointed in how a date worked out?" or "When you're with that person, how do you feel?" These questions may make it easier for kids to talk about their experiences.

We can convey some degree of personal experience if it seems right. We could convey a story of wanting to be more intimate with someone who said no and how that felt. Or a story of wanting to say no but feeling persuaded or pressured to say yes. We know how important it is for our kids to communicate clearly - no matter which role they are in at the moment. We know this is challenging. We may have bumbled through adolescence and young adulthood (not to mention older adulthood). Let them know this can be messy and confusing and wonderful and exciting. We hope they consider us a reasonable source if they need advice, support, or guidance.

Here is what I learned from training in martial arts and teaching self-defense to women for several years. I say it like this to the 8th graders, and I said it very clearly to both of our children: "If you've conveyed in every way you can that you want someone to stop or leave you alone and they aren't listening or responding, your next step is to escalate the situation. If clear, direct words aren't working, raise your voice and start shouting. Yell for help. Shout as loud as you can, "You're hurting me!" If yelling doesn't work, you have permission to push them away, hit them, or use any physical force available." In a self-defense class, we teach simple things people can do even if they are weaker than the person they're dealing with. We also tell them that resisting with their voice and body discourages the person who isn't listening and is trying to hurt them.

Talk about being sexual with others in general.

Being sexual can mean all kinds of things to all sorts of people. It can be about generating more love. It can be the mysterious cohesive force in long-term relationships.

Being sexual with someone can also be transactional. People can agree to have sex, and both people understand the transaction. People can purchase sex both online and in person. When we let them know we know about all of this, they might be able to ask questions or even talk about their experiences in the world.

Talk about making babies.

When a young person asks where babies come from, we can say, "Great question. Let me be sure I understand what you're asking." Your job at this moment is not necessarily to tell them all about penis-in-vagina sex. Your job at this moment is to gather a bit more information about what they are asking. They're not necessarily asking how babies are made; they may simply be asking where babies come from. Maybe all they need is "from your mother" or "inside a person's body ." If they want more information than that, they'll ask. Then, by all means, tell them more.

Before puberty, most kids will interpret what we say literally, so we must be thoughtful about our chosen words. Rather than talking about body parts they use for urination, we create a context that makes sense to them - people in relationships. They understand relationships.

Babies grow inside someone's body. The uterus, not the belly, is where babies grow. If they ask for more, we find ways to explain how a baby might be growing inside someone. We say something about how some adults build relationships that support a baby (whether there is a guardian, one parent, or many parents, there are relationships that support the baby). We remind them of the different kinds of relationships they already have with friends and family. We mention the skills they've developed in navigating those relationships.

"In some adult relationships, some adults can make babies! And that's how a baby can be inside of someone; it's amazing, isn't it!" Depending on the particular child and their developmental age, that might answer their question. If they're curious for more, we continue.

"How does the baby get inside?" they might ask.

"You know how we like to watch plants grow from seeds? Well, a baby grows similarly. It's not the same, but babies do start small and grow bigger while still inside the mother."

"How does the seed get inside?"

"Well, it's amazing. And it's a little complicated. To answer this, I will be talking about human bodies and how we reproduce. Shall we keep going? This is a great topic. We can keep talking about it or come back to this later."

If they're still eager for more, you could say:

"You know how some people have penises, and some people have vaginas? Well, human bodies can do surprising things. Male bodies produce tiny cells called sperm. They are tiny, one-celled creatures, tinier than anything you can see with your eyes. Sperm live in a thick fluid we call semen, which we can see. Female bodies are born with tiny cells called ovum tucked into their ovaries, which are inside their body. If the ovum welcomes the sperm, this new combination of ovum and sperm makes an embryo. That tiny, almost invisible embryo slowly grows inside the uterus for almost a year. Eventually, the baby is ready to live outside the mother's body. Isn't that amazing?"

If they are still curious, you could say:

"You might already know that penises can be soft and penises can become firm. You might not know that vaginas can be dry inside or moist and slippery inside. When people are older - teenagers and adults - they find ways for the penis to fit into the vagina. It may be confusing since, right now, you pee from your penis/vagina. Sometimes touching your vagina/penis can feel good. That's part of people fitting their bodies together. It can feel really good. A penis can become quite firm, and a vaginal canal can become quite slippery so they can bring their bodies together. Hopefully, this will feel good to both people. When it feels especially good, our bodies do some-thing called "orgasm," and that means we let a wave of really, really good feelings sweep through our bodies. When a person with a penis has an orgasm, the "seeds" we call sperm come out through the penis. Yes, humans pee through their penis, also. The body is amazing, and there is a valve that controls the small tube inside the penis that allows urine or sperm to come out. Only one tube can open at a time. Once the sperm (we call seed) are in the vaginal canal, a few of them find their way to the ovum (we call the egg). The egg admits only one sperm. This is what starts a baby growing. I'm happy to answer more questions. I also just gave you a lot of new information. Can we talk about that so I know I told the story clearly?"

The important thing here is that we take our cues from their questions.

If they stop after our first answer, we stop, too.

Hopefully, those few minutes will be pleasant instead of awk-ward, creating a sense of connection, curiosity, and even awe rather than discomfort. When they want more information or to challenge your answers, they will be comfortable asking. You're modeling a type of respectful connection. You're setting a pattern for many years of brief, age-appropriate conversations. There is no need to overwhelm them with information that will be baffling now but make sense later.

Talk about penis-body intercourse specifically.
My favorite phrase when approaching private topics with my teenagers was, "Hypothetically if someone were to...what would be important to know?"
As in, "Hypothetically, if two people want to enjoy any type of penis-body intercourse, what would be important to know?"
Your teenager might or might not tolerate you talking about this.
You might be certain you should talk about this, and your parenting partner might be just as certain you should not. Proceed with care.
Maybe we talk about sexual arousal cycles and how female bodies differ from male bodies. Perhaps we talk about the clitoris and its role in sexual pleasure. Maybe we should mention different forms of lubrication depending on the "hypothetical sexual activity" being discussed. This information is available on various educational platforms like scarleteen.com. and in many books written to educate and inform young people. (See Resources) Many kids will be more comfortable learning about this from someone besides their parents.

Talk about contraception and screening for STIs. I don't think talking with kids about sex or birth control will encourage them to be more sexual. I believe it will empower them to be smarter and safer when they are sexually active. (Data from other countries confirms this).

People engaging in genital sex involving male and female genitalia need to know that birth control methods exist, are affordable, and are obtainable at their local drug store. They need to know condoms are effective IF THEY USE THEM PROPERLY EVERY SINGLE TIME. They also need to have access to better methods of contraception if relevant. If you can be supportive of your adolescent being sexually active, help them access whatever form of birth control and protection is appropriate.

They also need to know that getting screened for Sexually Transmitted Infections is relatively easy and essential. The most common STI, chlamydia, has zero initial symptoms, can be cured with antibiotics (yes, cured, not just managed), and if left to prosper in your body, may cause infertility. Chlamydia is very common on college campuses, so don't hesitate to help them be well-informed before they leave home.

A good habit to encourage in your kids is to get tested every time they change sexual partners. Or, if that feels too awkward, you might suggest they get screened once or twice a year, just like they go to the dentist or the doctor.

Talk explicitly about the risks and pleasures of particular sexual behaviors. I include a blunt letter to a teenager who isn't speaking with you about any of this.

If you're living with a young person who appears to be very interested in, if not actively engaged in, some forms of sexual activity, you may want to try to convey a couple of key ideas. Especially if you'd prefer they abstain from particular activities for now.

Invite them to consider the relationship between pleasure and risk. (See Chapter 3, Sex is about Pleasure and so much more, and Chapter 9, Our Favorite Sex Ed Classes)

Once this is clear to them, they can hopefully enjoy intimate sexual activities that might include orgasms while delaying genital, oral, or anal sex until they're better able to mitigate the risks of pregnancy and sexually transmitted infections consistently. This is just fancy talk for using condoms or other forms of protection every single time they allow or put a penis into a body!

I offer the following letter to parents or teachers concerned about a young person's well-being and uncertain about what to do next. It provides brief, accurate information to help a sexually active young person avoid as much risk as possible.

Please use it as is or change it however you wish. If you are sure these conversations are impossible right now with your teenager, consider leaving this book and a few others around. I especially like Rethinking Sex by Christine Emba as an intro-duction to the current realities of dating. The author is about 30 years old.

I also like Erika Moen's books:

Drawn to Sex: Our Bodies, The Basics, Vol. 1, Limerence, 2018.

Drawn to Sex: Our Bodies and Health, Vol 2. Limerence Press, 2020.

Let's Talk About It: The Teen's Guide to Sex, Relationships, and Being a Human (A Graphic Novel) Random House Graphic, 2021

Also, scarleteen.com is Heather Corinna's incredibly well-informed and thorough website for young people.

If you are concerned about your teenager's sexual activity right now but can't imagine a conversation, this letter and these resources may help.

Dear _____,

I want you to be able to enjoy sexual relationships.

Sexual relationships are potent and pleasurable and potentially risky, but so are lots of things. You can enjoy the pleasurable parts and minimize the risky parts. I'm breaking it down here in terms of how much risk and how much pleasure is possible with various sexual activities.

Lower Risk and High Pleasure: *You know that orgasm is the peak of sexual pleasure. You may know that orgasm can be very different for different people. I encourage you to learn about the differences between people with a penis and people with a vulva. Search scarleteen.com for orgasm.*

You may also know that it is pretty standard for people to have orgasms without having penis-in-body intercourse. Fingers, hands, and mouths can stimulate orgasm.

Here is a simple guideline for avoiding pregnancy and infections:

1. *Enjoy the pleasurable ways to be together that may involve orgasm but do not involve the life-altering risks of starting a pregnancy or sharing infections.*
2. *Do not put a penis into another person's body anywhere without a condom on the penis.*
3. *Do not allow a penis into your body anywhere (vagina, anus, mouth) without a condom on the penis.*

Search scarleteen.com or plannedparenthood.com for more information.

Higher Risk and High Pleasure: *If you are going to enjoy penis-in-body sexual activity, it's even more important to be proficient with consent and condoms.*

Consent: *Consent is complicated.*

First, you have to pay attention to two things at once: how you feel and how the other person might feel.

Second, you have to communicate your feelings clearly (verbally or non-verbally) while also attending to communication (verbal or non-verbal) from the other person.

Third, you have to change your action based on that communication. If you realize your partner is uncomfortable, you know how to pause, adjust, or stop. If you are uncomfortable, you know how to make your partner pause, adjust, or stop.

If you can do those three things, making pre-sex agreements is still a good idea.

If you can't do those three things, you must make pre-sex agree-ments. You should also know those agreements can change at any moment.

Assuming the sexual activity you've seen online is "what people do" is a big mistake.

Assuming someone wants to do what you want - without asking them - is a dangerous mistake.

Assuming someone knows what you want to do and not do - without telling them - is also a dangerous mistake.

Be aware of legal definitions around failing to respond when someone asks you to stop, or you ask someone to stop. You can search for definitions of acquaintance rape, sexual harassment, and sexual assault.

Sexual Assault: *If you are uncomfortable with something that is happening and the person you are with isn't listening to you, I encourage you to be more forceful with your words and actions. Say "STOP". If that doesn't work, yell "STOP" and "HELP" as loud as possible. If necessary, use physical force - shove, kick, hit, run - to get them to stop touching you. If you have to be this force-ful with someone, they are harming you and committing sexual assault.*

Condoms and Lubrication: *If you decide to have penis-in-body sex, know that contrary to what you might hear, condoms are wonderfully effective (98%) when used correctly every single time but less effective (85%) due to human error. Using a con-dom only occasionally is an excellent way to start a pregnancy or share an infection.*

Search plannedparenthood.com for the effectiveness of condoms.

Here is a big box of condoms and a tube of lube. If you're sharing these with your friends (or not), leave the condom box or tube of lube where I will see them. I will refill them without questions. Even if you are already familiar with condoms, please read the instructions carefully. Sloppy use of condoms is a common cause of pregnancy and transmission of STIs.

If the person with the penis declines the use of the condom, you can decline participation. If you are a person with a penis, consider that wearing a condom might allow you to enjoy the sexual experience longer since it reduces the intensity. If someone doesn't want to use a condom, ask why. I hope you would insist on using a condom every time, for both of your sakes. Practice putting on a condom, no matter your genitals. Be good at it. That's why this is a big box of condoms, which I will refill without questions.

Chlamydia and HIV/AIDS: *As you know, making a mistake with a condom might mean getting or giving a sexually transmitted infection. Some have no early symptoms but are easily treated with antibiotics. This is why its important to routinely get tested. Planned Parenthood provides this and its not a big deal.*

Search on planned parenthood.com

Getting tested: *Health care providers suggest you get tested every six months as well as any time you are having sexually intimate contact with a new partner. Please set up an appointment with Planned Parenthood or with our doctor. You will not surprise any healthcare provider by telling them you're enjoying a sexual relationship, no matter your age. They help young*

people all the time. Their job is to help people seeking contra-
ception and treatment for STIs. Don't hesitate to tell them what
is true and ask any questions. If you're over 13, they won't have
to inform me. If I get a bill, I will pay it without asking questions.

Please use our doctor or a clinic where you feel comfortable to
get tested for sexually transmitted infections regularly.

Here is the phone number of a sexual health provider near you:

_____

Here is contact info for local clinics: _____

Planned Parenthood is a national organization and will answer
any questions. 1-800-230-7526.

Scarleteen is another excellent online resource about life, love,
and sexuality.

I assume you and I will not be talking about this, but I hope
this letter will make a conversation possible. Let me know if you
would like to talk more about this with someone in the family, a
counselor, or a healthcare person, and I will arrange it. Most of
all, this lets you know I am more interested in your well-being
than in maintaining rules. With love."

If it seems correct to you, deliver the big box of condoms, a
tube of lubrication, plus the letter (or even this book) to the
young person. You may disagree with what I say here, but still
accept that this may help a young person avoid the most life-
altering risks of specific sexual activity.

In some circumstances, this letter may lead to a conversation. Unfortunately, in some circumstances, it won't make any difference. Even if they ignore this completely, you have done what you could, and sometimes, that is all we can do.

Talk about your hopes for them.

If you can, take some time and figure out what you hope for each of your children.

Think about general hopes you might have for their experience of intimacy and connection with other humans. You aren't addressing anything specific about their body or their behaviors. You're talking about your hopes for their future, meaningful, intimate relationships.

Figure out how you want to say it. You could write it down if the conversation feels too awkward or like it will never happen. You use your creativity and resourcefulness in other areas of your life; you can also use them here. They will read what you write, listen to what you say, and want to know. That doesn't mean they will let you know this, nor does it mean they will do what you say.

But what you say matters deeply to them. So let them know.

We all learn about physical touch and intimacy from our caregivers - guardians, relatives, or parents. Our relationship with our kids is part of their understanding of and experience of intimacy. As they become young adults, they may want to experience closeness and connection of a different sort with people outside of the family with whom they may feel romantic or sexual attraction. These relationships are very different from family intimacy but have shared roots. Because of the shared roots, they bring the exact skills they've used in family and friendships into more sexually intimate relationships.

They know they can decide who they spend time with. They know they can say yes and tell someone they'd like to go out, kiss, or be more intimate. They know they can say no and tell someone to step back, back off, or stop touching them. They remember it's okay to be honest about what they want and what they don't want. They remember that other people have that right, too.

Since you've provided names for some of the general experiences they may have, they will be more able to speak about them with you as needed. We do this to help our kids develop strong, nourishing, vital relationships with their fellow human beings. Sometimes, those relationships involve sexual intimacy; sometimes, they don't. Sometimes, those relationships will be about something other than love or intimacy but simply about sharing pleasure. What matters is that they know they can ask us for help if needed. And they know how to care for themselves in whatever relationships they choose.

While this can all be a bit uncomfortable, I hope I've made my case for tolerating discomfort and doing our best to have these conversations with our kids. We are emphasizing the joy and complexity of intimacy as the foundation for solid and nourishing, sexual relationships.

MY FAVORITE SEX ED CLASSES

My husband and I developed our sex ed curriculum for 12-14-year-olds based on our counseling practices and his twenty years of teaching Human Relations at a small independent middle school. We attended an Our Whole Lives training as well. I worked with women recovering from sexual assault. My husband worked with adolescent boys. We knew we had to build the curriculum around the concept of consent. We also knew that simply teaching or talking about consent wouldn't be sufficient. We had to engage students' bodies and minds. We set up experiential exercises designed to engage students in understanding and practicing the subtle layers of self-awareness and consent necessary for healthy relationships.

We assumed most of our students were at least beginning to experience some form of sexual curiosity, if not sexual activity. We wanted them to know how to manage themselves as sexual beings. We wanted them to avoid harming or being harmed by others.

Teaching Sex Ed at an independent middle school allowed us to teach in particular ways.

We could talk about the importance of intimate or sexual interactions being comfortable and pleasurable for both people.

We could talk about how it feels when they aren't and the bad stuff that can happen. We could talk about protecting themselves and their partner from infection and, if relevant, pregnancy. We didn't lead with our fears for their safety or with the dangers of sex. We didn't emphasize risk, rules, restrictions, or reproduction. We didn't presume their ignorance. We didn't presume heteronormative, monogamous relationships.

Instead, we focused on the skills necessary to enjoy the pleasures and the risks of sexually intimate relationships without attempting to control their identity or their behavior. We also knew that simply talking about these things was just the beginning.

We always met with the parents to review the syllabus before we met with the students. We asked, "How many of you want your kids to be in good, nourishing, intimate, and sexual relationships during their lives?". Eventually, their hands began to go up. We asked them to write down their hopes for the sexual lives of their children on index cards. We gathered and mixed these up. We then invited each parent to pick an anonymous card and read it to all of us. Imagine. We also requested that they find a way to discuss their hopes with their kids.

On the first day of class with the eighth graders, we also asked, "How many of you want to be in good, nourishing, intimate, and sexual relationships in your life?" Each student took a little longer to figure out what we were asking. Slowly, the hands began to go up. We let them know we asked their parents the same question. We did not ask them to write about their hopes, but we did ask them to talk with their parents about this.

As parents, we might say that good sexual relationships can be one of the best parts of an adult life. We could speak of the powerful force of good sex while also conveying the risks and challenges. We could mention that sexual attraction happens in lots of different ways and that sexual relationships continue to grow and change throughout a lifetime. We could discuss how to develop, nourish, and maintain these relationships. We must talk about recognizing when relationships are nourishing and destructive.

We developed various teaching exercises.

Here are some examples. Please feel free to adapt and develop these ideas.

Experiential Exercises for Teaching Important Ideas

Consent: Invite and Decline

With younger kids, we open a discussion about dating. What might you want to do on a date? Where might you go? How would you ask? How would you accept or decline?

Then we talk about how to ask and decline an invitation.

We role-play passivity, assertiveness, and aggressiveness in asking for and rejecting something. Then, we model clear and respectful invitations and clear and respectful responses. We model and discuss unclear invitations and unclear responses. We point out condescending, hurtful invitations and responses. We talk about "being nice" and saying yes to avoid hurting someone's feelings as a type of lying. We encourage them to be clear and respectful in both inviting and declining.

Consent: Claim your Boundary

We do a version of this with each grade layering in complexity each year.

We ask them to form two lines, facing one another, like a line dance. We establish rules ensuring no one walks into anyone else.

First, person A walks towards person B until person B says, "Stop."

Second, we ask them to do the same exercise but add different walking styles. For example, we ask them to walk in a hesitant, avoidant, or distracted manner or a hurried, directed, or even aggressive manner.

We reverse roles and change partners regularly. Sometimes, if necessary, we separate two kids who can't seem to manage the exercise.

After each "walk," we engage the kids in conversation about their experiences in each role. We might comment on how the dynamics varied between each pair. Every year, there would be the kid who never said: "stop." They would declare, "I'm fine; I don't have any boundaries." We wouldn't argue but hope for another opportunity to explore this with them.

Consent: Persuasion or Coercion?

We talk about the variety of personal styles involved in inviting and declining. We talk about how subjective these styles are and how easy it is to misunderstand someone. We draw a line on the board and ask them to name the range of behaviors from invite to force. They tend to be invited, persuaded, pressured, coerced, and forced. We encourage them to recognize their style and to realize how easy it is to misinterpret another person's behavior. One person's eager and exuberant persuasion might feel like uncomfortable pressure or even coercion. One person's silence might be confused with agreement.

When is hinting more like asking?

When is asking more like persuasion?

When is persuasion more like coercion?

When is coercion more like blackmail?

When is blackmail more like force?

When is force essentially assault?

It's no surprise that they fully understood the two opposite ends of the spectrum. The complexity and nuance arise from the subjectivity of personal experience and expression.

We want students to know how to invite someone to come closer and ask someone to step back. They should be precise (no ambiguous passivity) and respectful (no coercion or insulting). We encourage them to be as transparent as possible about what they want and don't want in relationships.

We taught different material to 6th graders than we did to 8th graders, but the core principles of self-awareness and consent were consistent.

The Pleasure:Risk Ratio

We want to be sure students and kids understand the correlation between pleasure and risk. A great deal of pleasure is possible with relatively little risk of infection or pregnancy.

When they are relatively new to being sexual, it is crucial to help them figure out how to manage the pleasurable parts and minimize the risky parts.

Ejaculation of semen that is free of any infections or diseases will not spread sexually transmitted infections. Bodily fluids alone are not a problem.

The problem is that the most common sexually transmitted infections don't cause noticeable symptoms immediately. Often, people don't know there is a problem until the disease has progressed. If two people are getting tested regularly and are confident neither is the unfortunate recipient of an infection, they only need to protect against pregnancy, if relevant.

However, because infections are often invisible and because people do not tend to get tested regularly, a good general rule is not to allow sperm into a body.

As long as semen doesn't enter the throat or the vulva, or the anus, there is little risk of transmitting infection or disease.

As long as semen doesn't enter the vaginal canal, there is little risk of pregnancy.

These are general guidelines that a young person might consider until they can consistently use the necessary protection. In general, people can experience orgasm without sharing bodily fluids. This means that much pleasure is possible with relatively little risk.

After ten years of standing before children and parents and discussing all this, I am desensitized to this blunt language. I don't imagine you will use this exact language with your children. However, clear and concise guidelines are critical in early sexual activity.

Low and High Risk

We developed a class for 8th graders, teaching them to identify the difference between low and high-risk sexual activity in direct relationship to pleasure and orgasm. In the Our Whole Lives curriculum, they called this "Outercourse." I couldn't use this term, but I appreciated the concept.

On the whiteboard, I drew four columns. We asked the students what their categories were for gradually increasing intimacy.

We titled the columns something like Early Dating, Making Out, Fooling Around but Not sex, and Sex.

The more vocal kids eagerly described what tended to happen in each phase. There was usually much laughter and general agreement about the first two columns. When they stumbled over descriptions for Making Out and "Fooling Around but not Sex, I'd usually offer "above clothes and above the waist" for Making Out and "below the waist and below clothes" for Fooling Around. (Imagine the giggles!)

We set them up to disagree about the placement of Oral Sex. Was oral sex, sex or not? It usually ended up on the line between Not Sex and Sex. They could quickly agree that penis-vagina penetration and penis-anal penetration were sex. They always argued about Oral Sex - which was our intention.

I would also ask about pleasure and orgasm potential in each column. We would then invite them to notice the minimal risks in the first column and the mild risks but high potential for pleasure in the second and third columns. People can enjoy maximum pleasure with minimum risk doing all kinds of things that aren't intercourse.

As you increase pleasure and risk, you want to be confident in managing that risk. The next layer of this class considered the risks involved with the behaviors in each column. We started with the social risks.

Social risk.

Would you feel comfortable telling your friends about what you're doing?

Will you be comfortable tomorrow when you see this person in the hall?

Will they talk about your relationship with their friends?

Would you be comfortable if your parents knew what you're doing?

Personal risk.

Can you trust this person to be truthful about what they want and don't want?

Do you trust they will be respectful and kind to you and not be intrusive or manipulative?

Can you trust them to tell you if/when they change their mind about your relationship?

Can you be transparent with them about what you want and don't want? Do they listen?

Will they be honest with you about their feelings and what matters to them?

Physical and medical risk.

Are you sharing body parts that transmit diseases more severe than the flu?

Safe: mouth to mouth, hands to the outside of body, including genitals.

Risky: mouth to genital, genital to genital, mouth to anus, genital to anus.

Are you using latex properly if you are doing anything risky?

If pregnancy/paternity is a possibility, are you protecting against it every single time?

Do you know your partner's sexual history? With whom have they been sexual? Do you trust they are honest with you about this? Were their previous partners tested for sexually transmitted infections? Would they know? Has sufficient time passed for symptoms to be known?

Could you tell them if something happened that felt uncomfortable, invasive, or just bad? If not, could you tell someone you trust to help you figure out what happened and what to do next?

It is okay to ask all of these questions. I wouldn't require answers. Depending on so many variables, asking and trying to have these tough conversations could be difficult.

We don't hesitate to talk about how to drive in the snow. We tell kids again and again not to drive when intoxicated. We can be just as specific with sexual intimacy. We aren't trying to stop them. We are giving them information so they can make decisions on their own. They may realize they want to be in relationships where they can ask these questions and trust the person's answers.

Encouragement to be blunt

Orgasms can happen with hands. No one will get pregnant, nor will an STI be transmitted. Mouths and throats, vaginal canals, and rectums can be infected by sperm. If someone wants to enjoy penetrative oral, genital, or anal sex with a penis, they need to be a skillful condom user. Condoms work well but only when used correctly every single time.

Both people should get tested every 6 -12 months. The most prevalent sexually transmitted infections are treatable with one round of antibiotics. (See Chapter 3, Sex is about pleasure and so much more)

Teaching Anatomy and Physiology of sexual pleasure and reproduction

We can teach the physiology of sexual pleasure as well as sexual reproduction.

When teaching, we used 20-year-old anatomical diagrams displaying "male and female reproductive anatomy." They included add-ons for female and male anatomy. The female diagram's add-ons included ovulation, menstruation, and gestation images. The male diagram's add-ons included images of sperm and an erect penis. This made it easy to explain the physiology of male sexual arousal and ejaculation.

There was no add-on erect clitoris, so there was no discussion of female sexual arousal, lubrication of the muscular walls of the vaginal canal, or female orgasm. The clitoris isn't necessary for sexual reproduction, but perhaps that isn't the only reason it wasn't included since the rectum and intestines were included.

It took us too long to overcome our embarrassment and point this out to the students. For too many years, we never even spoke of women's orgasms.

We can teach about the variability in sexual organs.

Once we are teaching our kids to be wise and capable sexual beings, we can also teach about the variability in sexual organs. In utero, the physiology of the genitals share a basic template. The clitoris and the penis arise from the same embryological template that shifts and changes depending on chromosomes and hormones. During the first six weeks of fetal development, all fetuses are female. The basic shape and key elements of gonads (ovaries or testes), erectile tissue (clitoris or penis), and a concentration of nerve endings are quite similar. We come from the same stuff. The shape and function of that same stuff varies even within genders.

We can teach about genitals, genders, and sexual orientation.

Genitals don't determine gender. Gender doesn't determine genitals. Neither genitals nor genders determine sexual attraction. Sexual attraction itself isn't assumed. We use language that deliberately talks about humans - rather than language that assumes anything. We discuss how humans may be attracted to one another and may want to share pleasure. We avoid language that limits sexual activity to female-male genital intercourse. We talk about sexual relationships in ways that include pleasure while also being transparent about the specific risks of specific sexual activities.

When we lead with this, young people tend to listen.

CHAPTER

10

PARENTING PROSPECTIVE ADULTS

In general, we parents are the ones most able to change our minds. Our brains are fully developed. We have years of experience navigating life. We can modulate and regulate big, intense feelings. We can put things in perspective. We can think before we speak.

At least most of the time.

Compared to our children, we are far more capable of changing our behavior than they are. If there's a problem, we are the ones who can shift our attitude, strategy, and behavior.

At least most of the time.

While they live with us, they are the child. The child gets to be who they are, given their age. They get to bumble along in a developmentally appropriate manner. There will be a difference between how we parent a three-year-old, a 13-year-old, a 16-year-old, and a 23-year-old. Each age is good preparation for the next, and each age will stretch our ability to adapt to this ever-more-independent human.

It's hard to remember that we are raising prospective adults.

We know they are not yet adults. Their brains will fully function once they are 23 - 25 years old. When and how do we shift from parenting a little kid to parenting a new adult who will soon live independently?

Once upon a time, your child was truly a child. That snuggly toddler now resists your hugs. That curious child now looks elsewhere for answers. They are in the middle of an internal hurricane, and our job - however daunting - is to guide them through the tumult of their teenage years steadfastly.

At least, that's how I thought about adolescence.

We are wrong if we think our kids are the only ones going through significant changes.

Our bodies are aging while theirs are blossoming. Our inner world is full of questions just like theirs.

Let's consider this transition from parenting children to parenting new adults.

At the beginning, we are solely responsible for keeping this tiny, helpless being alive. Within what seems a very short time, we must step aside and watch them begin to lead. Everyone involved in this transition will make mistakes. Tempers will flare; tender hearts will be hurt. What we can do is make room for this. Expect it. Remind ourselves relationships get strained just like muscles. Just like muscles, we must attend to the strain before it worsens. Rupture, then repair. Disagree, then get curious about why and try to learn from the disagreement. We may need to be less involved in every single decision. They need to practice making their own decisions.

Idealized parents

We can help with humble, honest tracking of our lives in this transitional time. Who am I, as a parent at this moment? How is my life going? What transitions am I in?

As long as we appear fine, we essentially insert an 'idealized parent avatar' into our kids' inner world. They feel vulnerable all the time. We can let them know we feel vulnerable, too. This is not an invitation to expect our kids to be our best friends. This is an invitation to offer the occasional headline judiciously.

Share vulnerability

It might sound something like this:

"I got angry last night. I wasn't thinking very clearly. Can we discuss that again now that I'm not so angry?"

We can admit mistakes and share doubts.

"I lost my job. I'm talking with friends about what to do next, but I wanted you to know."

"I'm exhausted, but I haven't figured out why. I'm sorry I can't be at that event."

We are revealing our vulnerability. We aren't asking our teens to solve anything.

We might also share a few judicious headlines of mistakes from our younger years.

"I ended up in a bad situation when I was younger. I wish I'd known better how to handle it."

"I had many friends and did well in school, but I wasn't being true to myself."

"I was hungry all the time and bullied the weak kids at school for their lunch."

We offer headlines, not the full article. If they want to hear more, they will ask. Honesty infused with humility is powerful. We can offer this.

Age-Perception Dissonance

Another challenge for parents of older kids is "age-perception dissonance." We see them as children, and they experience themselves as soon-to-be adults.

From my vantage point, the world began the moment I was born.

However old I was, I was as old as I'd ever been, so that was pretty grown up. Remember how cool it was to be so grown up? No matter what age you were, you felt so much more grown-up than you'd ever felt before. Remember how it felt when your parent(s) didn't recognize your newfound maturity?

One reason kids stop talking to their parents is the dissonance between how mature they perceive themselves to be and how mature we perceive them to be. We must give them room to find their way while coaching them toward their independent young adulthood.

We forget our adolescence.

Ask yourself gently what you remember.

What was good about those years, and what was challenging?

What did you figure out on your own?

When did you realize how you were different from or similar to your parents?

What kind of a teenager were you?

Are there any similarities between you as a teenager and the current teenager living in your house?

How did your parents respond when you made mistakes?

How did that feel to you?

How did you handle conflict?

Were you eager to leave home, or did it feel too soon?

Given all of this, could we approach raising older children differently?

What would a new baby's parents need to do to smoothly transition from parenting an infant to shepherding a new adult into the world? Once kids become teens, they are only a few years away from living independently.

If you were this project's manager, how might you plan for it?

How would you prepare yourself and your teenager for independence?

We've acknowledged that we adults are immersed in our journeys and bring our quirks to this relationship. We've noted the problem with age perception dissonance. We may also be feeling less confident in our brilliant parenting skills. The rules that made sense a while ago may not make sense today. And our kids will likely be sliding around those rules more than we realize.

In a room with about 30 high school kids, we asked, "How many of you have lied to a parent?" Fairly exuberantly, all hands went up. The prevailing attitude was, "Of course we do, and we're kind of proud of it."

Teenagers will do what is needed to bond with their peers. Many teenagers are good at resourceful and imaginative ways to elude parental attempts at control. Many teenagers are perfectly comfortable lying.

Kids will find a way to do what they want, even if they must lie. Some will never challenge you directly, and some will constantly challenge you. There will be that moment when your rules significantly damage their sense of dignity and place with their peers. Then, they will find a way around them.

We may respond to this with a reflexive increase of restriction or punishment in yet another attempt to control behavior. At some point in our righteous indignation, we realize we are losing contact with our teenager. When we suspect our kid is not being entirely truthful, we might have to accept that it's time for a significant transition in parenting.

I don't know when the change needs to happen in your household. Often the pressure is building significantly between sophomore year and graduation from high school. Teens reach this developmental shift at various ages. Some arrive sooner than expected, while others arrive later. No matter when they get there, we have to adapt when they do. Conflict escalates, trust disintegrates, and relationships deteriorate when we don't.

The shift from rules to truth

Can we shift from "These are the rules, and you must follow them until you leave home (and even after)" to "I would like to change how I've been parenting. I'd like to shift from "parental rules" to "mutual understandings. I realize our rules are too constricting, so you've had to maneuver and lie. I'd feel better knowing what you're doing so we could talk about it. I'd feel better if our relationship was as honest as we can manage now."

We can offer fewer restrictions in exchange for more honest information about their lives. Knowing what they are doing will make our responses more relevant and valuable. We can offer our perspective on the situations they are navigating.

Now, we have to manage our responses. Instead of scolding, we try to ask genuinely respectful, inquiring questions. We help them think about the range of possible outcomes of particular decisions. When there's a problem to solve, what might they do next? We might even notice and appreciate an unexpected solution they suggest.

We don't just rescue them if protection or advocacy is needed. We ask what they want from us. We could provide coaching and step in if our help is still required. Let's stand aside, let them handle it, and discuss how it went. If something fails, we offer as much steady love and support as possible. If necessary, we may step in fully to protect them.

The benefit to the kids is evident.

The benefit to the parent is increased honesty in communication and a strengthened instead of a broken relationship. The major benefit is that if something truly dangerous is happening in their lives, they might be able to tell us and we might be able to help.

We can begin to explain ourselves at some point in this relationship with a new adult. We can let them know how particular circumstances affect us and ask how they affect them. We do our best to respect their opinions, and we can expect them to listen to ours but not necessarily agree.

As the new adult in your house leaves for the evening, you may say, "When do you think you'll be home?" Their first reaction will be, "Mom, you said you trusted me to make my own decisions now." At which point you say, "I do trust you. But I'm also taking care of myself. When I wake up at night, and you're not home, I worry about you, and then it isn't easy to get back to sleep. This is okay sometimes, but it's rough for me if I need to work the next day. Could we talk about ways you could let me know the basics of your plans?"

This is tricky because this sounds like a worried and controlling parent. The difference is that we ask for something to help us rather than manage their behavior.

How will we handle the inevitable disagreements when they come home to visit or stay while? How will we talk about what matters to each of us? How do we manage disagreements with our good friends? That's the quality of the relationship we're working towards. Respectful, clear communication while honoring differences.

We will have a relationship with this new young adult for much longer than we did with them as children.

Let's prepare and look forward to that. I want a good relationship with my kids for as long as we live. This means that at some point, I need to stop being the parent in charge who expects some form of agreement if not obedience. Instead, I must figure out how to step back, offer support, get out of their way, and stay present simultaneously!

"I don't know how to describe parenting when you're 22 and living at home again," Mom said to an adult daughter.

"Parenting isn't the right verb anymore," said the daughter to Mom.

Sometimes, we are just trying to keep our kids alive. Sometimes, the mysterious mix of genetic inheritance and life circumstances makes growing up even more challenging. As I write about this, I think of all the people I know and love who work hard to hold steady and get through a day.

I think of so many of us teetering between fear and despair.

I think of my cousin, who killed herself after asking for help.

I think of a young woman who tried to kill herself while also remembering her mother's words: "If you ever do try to kill yourself, get yourself to a hospital." This is precisely what she did.

I think of my brother-in-law, who disappeared for years until my husband found him living on the streets of Los Angeles.

I think of friends whose children discovered their tendency to become addicted - whether to alcohol or particular drugs, gaming or work, or sex.

I think of friends who sent their teenagers away for rehabilitation. However imperfect, it seemed safer than letting them stay at home.

Sometimes, our job becomes keeping our children alive.

I think of each of these challenges as a medical condition, much like diabetes. Not because there will necessarily be a medical solution but to help parents help their kids. If they were diagnosed with wildly fluctuating blood sugar, we would help them get insulin. If they broke their leg, we would take them to get a cast. If depression or anxiety were crippling them, could we find a good therapist and maybe a psychiatrist and see if medication might help? If alcohol became the main focus of their life, could we admit it and let them know we are ready to help in any way possible? Could we call friends who deal with addictions and ask for their guidance and help?

Can we tolerate what is true rather than holding onto what we wish were true?

Can we tolerate what is true and still be a steady, caring presence for this new adult?

I wonder if some of this would be easier if we paid less attention to a culturally defined idea of normal, much less success, and more attention to each person's particular abilities and tendencies. Can we be less concerned with how others might view us or our children and more concerned with their well-being?

Parenting is not a business transaction in which one person comes out ahead.

Parenting is utterly imperfect and messy and constantly humbling.

Our most important job now is to stop imposing our vision and instead be curious about theirs so we can offer them life-long love and support. Our best gifts are our presence, patience, and open-hearted tolerance if not acceptance. This looks wildly different in each family, but we can honor this new adult to the best of our ability.

The questions to work with now are:

Who is this new adult emerging before my eyes?

What can I provide - within the range of who I am?

What can they manage - within the range of who they are?

How can I nourish our bond for the rest of our lives?

AFTERWORD

When there are kids in the house, it feels like everything we say or do matters. It does, but only so much.

We played the genetic lottery and did our best from there, like all the parents before us, including our own.

We may be wise guides. We may think our teenagers should recognize the brilliance of our guidance and want to follow our maps.

Our job is not to teach them to follow our map. Our job is to step aside while they figure out their own internal guidance system. For some, the idea of a map won't even make sense. They may wander in ways that appear aimless to us. They may sense an inner guiding principle unknown to us. They may be in a 4-wheel drive, going exactly where they want to go.

Can we get out of their way, let them fly and fall, and assure them we are there when they need us?

As we listen to emerging wisdom, we realize there is no normal to which we should all aspire. We are each the result of the genetic lottery - neurologically, physiologically, and psychologically unique humans. We each find our way. Can we stop navigating towards an unreachable place called normal.

It doesn't exist.

That is a map to misery.

As our children leave home, it's time for us to reorient. Who are we now, and where are we going?

ACKNOWLEDGEMENT

Thanks go to all the humans throughout time and around the world who can share their ideas with the rest of us. I write out of the murky slurry of their ideas as I've absorbed, dissolved, and reconfigured them.

Thanks to each of the friends, family, and editors who said, "Keep going." Bless you, especially those who read entire manuscripts and helped me clarify the murk.

Thanks go especially to my long-haul husband, who steadfastly encourages, laughs, and thinks out loud with me.

All our former students - including our children - are living their adult lives in the world. To any students reading this, hello!

Kathie McCarthy, May, 2024

RESOURCES

For Parents and Teachers

Online Resources

Ang Fonte, Justine, M. Ed, MPH, Intersectional Health Education, *justinefonte.com*

Casper, Sarah, Consent Educator, *comprehensiveconsent.com*

Harwood, Eli, MA, therapist, *attachmentnerd.com*

Hodder-Shipp, Anne, CSE, ACS, Sex and Relationship Educator, *annhoddership.com*

Martin, Betty, Dr., The Wheel of Consent, *bettymartiin.org*

Our Whole Lives: Lifespan Sexuality Education, *UUA.org*

Planned Parenthood, *plannedparenthood.org*

Scarleteen, Sex Ed for the Real World, *scarleteen.com*

Sex Positive Families, *sexpositivefamilies.com*

Teach Us Consent, Australia, *teachusconsent.com*

Books

Orenstein, Peggy, *Boys & Sex: Young Men on Hookups, Love, Porn, Consent and Navigating the New Masculinity*. Harper, 2020.

Orenstein, Peggy, Girls & Sex: Navigating the Complicated New Landscape. Harper Collins, 2016.

On Pornography

Crabbe, M., & Flood, M. (2021). School-Based Education to Address Pornography's Influence on Young People: A Proposed Practice Framework. *American Journal of Sexuality Education, 16*(1), 1-37.

Herbenick, Debby, Phd., Stone, S. Esq., Supler, K. Esq., *Yes, Your Kid*. BenBella Books, 2023.

Orenstein, Peggy, *If You Ignore Porn, You Aren't Teaching Sex Ed*, NYTimes, June 14, 2021.

Orenstein, Peggy, *The Troubling Trend in Teenage Sex*, NYTimes, April 12, 2024.

Wilson, Gary, *Your Brain on Porn: Internet Pornography and the Emerging Science of Addiction*, Commonwealth Publishing, 2015.

For Young People

Bailar, Schuyler, *He/She/They*. Hachette Go, 2023.

Corinna, Heather, S.E.X., second edition: *The All You-Need-To-Know Sexuality Guide to Get You Through Your Teens and Twenties*. Da Capo Lifelong Books, 2016.

Corinna, Heather and Rotman, Isabella, *Wait, What? A Comic Book Guide to Relationships, Bodies, and Growing Up*. Limerence Press, 2019.

Hiddinga, Laura, *Are You Coming? A Vagina Owner's Guide to Orgasm*. The Experiment, 2021.

Kobabe, Maia, *GenderQueer, a Memoir*. Oni-Lion Forge Publishing, 2020.

Mady, G. and Zuckerberg, J.R., *A Quick and Easy Guide to Queer and Trans Identities*. Limerence Press, 2019.

Moen, Erika and Nolan, Matthew, *Drawn to Sex: Our Bodies, The Basics, Vol. 1*. Limerence, 2018.

Moen, Erika and Nolan, Matthew, *Drawn to Sex: Our Bodies and Health, Vol 2*. Limerence Press, 2020.

Moen, Erika and Nolan, Matthew, *Let's Talk About It: The Teen's Guide to Sex, Relationships, and Being a Human* (A Graphic Novel). Random House Graphic, 2021

Reynolds, Kate E., *What's Happening to Ellie? A book about puberty for girls and young women with autism and related conditions*. Jessica Kingsley, 2015.

Reynolds, Kate E., *What's Happening to Tom? A book about puberty for boys and young men with autism and related conditions*. Jessica Kingsley Publishers, 2015.

Rotman, Isabella, *A Quick & Easy Guide to Consent*. Limerence Press, 2020.

Sanders, Sue, *Mom, I'm Not a Kid Anymore: Navigating 25 Inevitable Conversations that Arrive Before You Know It.* The Experiment, 2013.

Silverberg, Cory, *You Know, Sex: Bodies, Gender, Puberty, and Other Things.* Triangle Square, 2022.

For Younger Kids

Harris, Robie, *It's so Amazing, and It's Perfectly Normal.* Candlewick Press, 2014.

Further Reading

Blair, Gabrielle, *Ejaculate Responsibly.* Workman Publishing, 2022.

Emba, Christine, *Rethinking Sex: A Provocation.* Sentinel, Penguin Random House, 2022.

hooks, bell, *The Will to Change: Men, Masculinity, and Love. Washington Square Press, 2004*

Jordan-Young, Rebecca, M., *Brain Storm: The Flaws in the Science of Sex Differences, Harvard University Press, 2011*

Mack, Marlo, *How to be a girl: A Mother's Memoir of Raising Her Transgender Daughter,* Workman Publishing, 2021.

Maté, Gabor, *The Myth of Normal.* Penguin, Random House, 2022.

Maté Gabor, *In the Realm of Hungry Ghosts: Close Encounters with Addiction.* Atlantic Books, 2010.

Nogaski, Emily, *Come as you Are.* Simon and Schuster, 2021.

Reese, Trystan, *How We Do Family: From Adoption to Trans Pregnancy What We Learned About Love and LGBTQ Parenthood.* The Experiment, 2021.

Roughgarden, J. *Evolution's Rainbow: Diversity, Gender, and Sexuality in Nature and People.* Berkeley CA: Univ. of California Press, 2004.

Roughgarden, J. *The Genial Gene: Deconstructing Darwinian Selfishness.* University of California Press, 2009

Riley, Cole Arthur, *This Here Flesh,* Convergent Books, Penguin, 2022.

Siegel, Dan, *Brainstorm: The Power and Purpose of the Teenages Brain.* TarcherPerigee, 2015.

Siegel, Dan, *Mindsight: The New Science of Personal Transformation.* Bantam, 2010.

Taylor, Sonya Renee, *The Body is not an Apology,* Berrett-Koehler Publishers, 2nd ed., 2021

Waeber, David and Wengrow, David, *The Dawn of Everything: A New History of Humanity.* Farrar, Straus and Giroux, 2021.

Whippman, Ruth, *BoyMom: Reimagining Boyhood in the Age of Impossible Masculinity*, Harmony, 2024.

ABOUT THE AUTHOR

Since 1980, McCarthy's work has emerged from deep roots of curiosity about the body as a source of power, pleasure, and wisdom. She counseled clients dealing with somatic symptoms of sexual trauma in the 1990s. In the early 2000s she taught Sex Education to parents and kids from elementary through high school. She trained and led older women on multi-day wilderness backpacking trips until 2019. She has worked with her hands as a massage therapist since 1980.

Listening as best she could to all the humans she encountered, inspired her to write this book. The persistent motivator was the annual question from an 8th-grade girl in Sex Education class: "Does sex hurt?" Reorienting the Sex Talk is McCarthy's best answer to a question no one should have to ask.

Printed in the USA
CPSIA information can be obtained
at www.ICGtesting.com
JSHW011433270924
70522JS00008B/200